Bubble

Copyright Bubble and Margot Bish 2025

The moral rights of Bubble and Margot Bish to be identified as the author of this work has been asserted in accordance with the Copyright Designs and Patent Act 1988. All rights reserved. No part of this publication may be reproduced, stored in a retrieval system or transmitted in any form or by any means without the prior permission of the copyright owners

Bubble

By

Bubble and Margot Bish

Introduction

Bubble and I have read over the last fourteen years many books about or written by cats, The Dalai Lama's cat
in particular influenced Bubble to ask if I might type her story for her.
When we first met in the cat sanctuary, her vocabulary consisted of many swear words and curses, her life experience for six months, the stories of other cats who shared the sanctuary but little else.

Since moving to live with me, an avid reader and more lately an author, her vocabulary and ability to communicate through telepathy have broadened to incredible standards.
There have been dramas aplenty with my adventurous independent thinking cat. I hope you enjoy reading about them.

24th October 2009

I was born in a stable, my first sounds, the beating of my mother's heart, the first smell, my mother's life giving milk as I crawled instinctively to the teat, but with my tummy full, my ears picked up more sounds, the rustle of straw, hooves scraping on concrete and the harrumphing snorts and whifflings of horse to horse overlaying my brothers and sisters' cries as they mewed for milk. My mother's rough tongue, cleaned my damp fur, a paw holding me still as I wriggled. Nostrils twitching, I was aware of horse manure and sweat, the mustiness of damp horse rug and the sweetness of saddle wax. Eyes tight shut, we listened, too to the song of wisdom, as passed from cat to kitten through the centuries, in my mother's purr. A song of survival. Trust only your instincts, beware of mankind, the pictures of prey and predator impressed on our minds as we lay in the curve of warm fur, a paw preventing us crawling too far from the safe cocoon. We felt secure and content, well fed and protected as our first night ticked by in the darkness of the stable.

25/10/2009

With morning came more noise. Buckets clattering, the voices of man calling to man, bolts thumping and doors opening, the rustle of boots through straw and then a sudden silence. I sensed my mother's head raised, wary and watching, and then a man's voice close by calling eagerly, and more boots thudded. Even with no sight, I could sense the awed ring of faces gazing down at us with delight and compassion, the voices hushed, and then an authoritative voice called from elsewhere and the ring broke up and faded from my awareness. There were thuds of hay bales and the clomp, clomp clomp as the horses were led away, leaving a draught from the open doors tickling our fur and bringing new unidentifiable smells.

This was my existence as weeks passed, the song vibrating from cat to kittens as we drank and slept, and then, our eyes opened and we saw the great beasts we shared the stable with, tolerant and peaceful. We saw rafters overhead and timber walls enclosed our world We clamoured for release from our mother's protective embrace, wriggling determinedly beyond her reach until she gave us our freedom to explore and satisfy our innate curiosity. We had great fun, climbing in the straw, leaping and falling as we learned how to use our stumpy tails for balance, play fighting, clambering up the harnesses and daring each other to balance on the rug covered rumps high above the ground., the rugs giving purchase, the smooth horses' coats slippery beneath our tiny paws.

It was a time of laughter and discovery that I wish could have been forever.

November / December

We were used to the coming and going of the stable lads, cleaning out the stalls around us, laughing and joking amongst themselves, taking the horses out for exercise, brushing out the autumn scents when they returned, easing the horses' powerful muscles and giving them feed. Gradually, our mother was adding raw rodents to our food. I much preferred the milk from the teat and mother would smile and say, "You'll never survive in the wild with your delicate tastes. We must find you a home with humans to feed you and your brothers and sisters who seem also to have unnatural tastes".

A few days later, strangers began to appear, crouching down to inspect us closely, snatching us up and turning us all ways up to check us over. I hated them all, especially the smallest with their "I want," whine and fingers that squeezed too tight. Gradually my siblings left us until only I and one sister were left, hiding under our mother whenever the doors were opened, creeping out when all was quiet again, but mother had to hunt, and the time came when she was not there to protect us. As we crouched in the straw, a family of three small people and two huge, shadowed over us, picked us up, looked carefully and took me away. I was clutched in tight, sticky fingers, my head almost buried in material that rubbed raw against my nose and eyes. There were metallic bumps and bangs and a loud cough and purr which I later learned was a car engine starting. I found my body moving of its own accord with jerks and moments of acceleration and deceleration that made me feel extremely sick. The small people argued and pulled at my body, all wanting to hold me at once until a deep growling voice reverberated from the front seats. "If you can't share quietly and fairly, we'll take her straight back and have no cat," and I found myself being passed from hand to hand like a bag of sweets, for the rest of the journey.

It ended at last and doors were opened. I was carried out, the breath being squashed from my lungs. There was a brief glimpse of a blue ceiling far, far above and bright golden light, and then we went into a building and I was plonked down on a hard wooden floor in the middle of a huge expanse of nothingness surrounded by cupboards all round the walls. There were shadows beneath and I streaked across the floor to hide in the deepest darkness where grasping hands, and even a broom handle could not reach me. I could smell and hear the snuffling of a dog somewhere close by and shivered at the thought of slavering teeth. I saw hands and knees and eyes peering into my gloomy space and sidled into the very corners of blackness.

"Leave her alone for now," a grown up female voice advised. "She'll come out when she sees there's nothing to be afraid of, or when she's hungry. How would you feel with so many eyes staring at you like a bunch of vultures at a feast?"

The querulous voices faded away, and I slipped forwards, my whiskers twitching to sense what this place was all about. It stank of wet dog and dog marking scents and disinfectant. Somewhere, a tap dripped, and light came in slantwise from a window showing the bareness of my prison – no softness, no straw, just hard, bare wood. I shivered. How could I escape? Had I heard enough of the song of wisdom to survive alone? My nose wrinkled at the thought of having to eat raw mouse and I wondered if I could even catch one. A door opened and I slid back into hiding. A dish of food and another of water were placed near me but so that I would have to come into the open to eat, and then a basket with a blanket also appeared. The lady's feet hovered, hopefully and then her face appeared looking sideways at me and fingers were offered for me to sniff.

"Please come out, little one," she said. "We want you to be part of our family, and you must eat." But I stubbornly stayed put until she sighed and went away.

Only when the house was quiet, with snores echoing from the floor above did I slip out to eat hurriedly and drink thirstily, sniffing the basket carefully and stepping into its warmth, but I cat napped with ears pricked, ready to bolt undercover at the smallest hint of danger, and was back in my hole when the family appeared, yawning and scuffling for breakfast.

"Well, she's been out and eaten, at least," the lady reassured her children. "School for you today, so maybe she'll come out when the house is quiet and decide it's not as frightening as she thought."

There were smells of cooking, and milk, the clattering of plates and cutlery. Feet seemed to be running in all directions, making the planks beneath my feet leap and bounce, children's voices bickered and doors opened and shut......and then there was silence. During all the chaotic movement, someone had put more food in my dish. I waited a while, straining my ears for sounds, but there was only the ticking of a clock and the hum of a refrigerator, sounds of constancy and reassurance. I crept out again and ate eagerly, lapped some water and then explored the whole room, making sure the door was shut, afraid of the scent of dog even in the silence. There was no way out. I found a box with some kind of sand in it and dug hastily, realising my bladder was crying to be emptied. At least I would be able to hide my smell as the song of wisdom advised. Tired out, I crawled into the basket, flopped on my side and slept.

When I awoke, the lady was sitting by the table, watching me. She smiled and greeted me in a gentle voice. "Hello little cat. You have nothing to fear, so please don't run and hide again."

I watched her carefully, suspiciously, but she made no sudden move, sitting relaxed in her chair. I turned myself to sit facing her, front paws tucked under my body, back legs tucked but ready to run and we watched each other curiously until my head began to nod and I slept again.

It was the thud of feet that woke me, and with my eyes barely open, I sprinted back under the cupboards. The lady sighed and got up, remonstrating, telling the children their rowdiness had sent me back into hiding, but it seemed impossible for them to be quiet and move without stomping and running. Days passed in a similar fashion.

I made friends with the lady, eventually sitting on her lap to be stroked and enjoying the strange new sensation, but the children terrified me, along with the smell of dog so strong in my nostrils even though I never saw the monster. I did gradually become used to the pattern of movement, no longer quivering with fear at the shouting and clattering when the children were home, but I still hid under furniture, watching them with big eyes, cautious of their grasping hands and chaotic movement, only relaxed in the mother's arms.

March 2010
One evening, with the children in bed, there was a serious discussion between the two adults, with glances at me, now lying in the

basket, and the next day, I was put in a cardboard box by the lady,. She looked unhappy.

"I've enjoyed your company," she said, "But this not the right home for you. I hope you find a better place to be."

She took me outside and I hoped, so hoped I was going back to my mother and the horses and the stable. I endured the sickening journey, thinking the frightening adventure would soon be over, but when I was lifted from the car, I was somewhere else. A kind of long shed with the smell of cats strong in the air. My new friend put a hand into the box and gave me a long rub around my ears and chin. And with a firming of the mouth, handed me to another lady, who took me through another door. With nightmarish horror, I saw row upon row of cats in small cages.

"Get away," one cried out to me. "Struggle and run while you can."

I wriggled in the hands that gripped me, trying to get leverage with my feet and claws but a cage door swung open, and I was placed inside with a pat on the head. The door swung shut. I could smell fear, desperation, rage and anger, emptiness and

loneliness, and perhaps most frightening failure and apathy. A face appeared at my level outside the bars and gazed compassionately at me. "Sorry my love," she said. "You have to stay here until we can find you a new home. I promise we will do it as quickly as we can."
She stuck a piece of paper on a board by the door of my cage and went away.

I could see some of the other cats press forward to look at me, all ages and colours, they studied me with frustration and compassion as I tried to get through the bars and escape from my unbearably small prison. I pawed at the walls and clung to the ceiling bars, trying to reach through and undo the bolt but it was all no good, and eventually I became aware of a telepathic voice in my mind. One of the other cats was singing to me as my mother had done, calming my mind, telling me to rest and I fell back on a cushion, exhausted.
"We've all tried," a war torn ginger tom told me, his voice rough and exasperated.
"There's only one way out of here, and that's dead."
"Oh Macallister," another voice admonished.

"You know that isn't true. Four cats this week have gone with people who chose them and took them to new homes."

"Huh," said Macallister, "That's alright for pedigrees....." he spat the word, "and cute little kittens, but not for us old ones."

"Well, there," said the calmer voice. "Look at her. She's almost a kitten herself, is she not?"

"Huh!" snorted Macallister, and turned his back on the world.

"My name is Maisie," the other voice told me, "Although they try to rename us here to forget our past, or some such rubbish, and yet my past was happy and I have no wish to forget it." She gave a half hiss. "I am now supposed to answer to Buttercup."

I thought of my mother and my brothers and sisters and realised we had not bothered with names. Labels had seemed unimportant as we played, ate and slept.

"What was your past?" I asked.

"I lived with a grand old lady for the whole of my life. I adored her, and she adored me, but last year, she was so ill she could no longer move without human help, and they took her away from our home. For a while, someone came and fed me and told me she was in hospital and might come home soon, but then the lady that fed me came one day and was crying, her face all blotchy and wet and she said my lady was not coming home again and I would have to go to a cat sanctuary where they would look after me until a new home was found for me. She put me in my travelling basket and brought me here, and they do look after us, despite what Mac says. Its just our independence we have lost, and of course, to a cat, that is everything."

I gazed at the other cats. "Do you all have pasts like that?" I asked.

"All different," a white cat said. "I had a whole family to look after. Three children and their mum and dad, but there was a day when they all looked worried because, they said, "Dad" had lost his job, and after that the house became cold when it had always been warm and Dad shouted and was angry all the time and Mum cried and my children that had almost always been happy were often sad. It seemed, after a while that they had to move out of our home and wherever they were going, I couldn't go with them, so I ended up here. I do miss them, and they all cried when they had to say goodbye to me. That cat in the corner, he lost his lady the same kind of way and he just sits now and gazes at the wall. He says his heart feels broken and his stomach full of glass. Doesn't even exercise when he is allowed in the run."

"What's the run?" I asked.

A black and white cat opposite indicated the corridor between the cages. "We take it in turns to be allowed to run up and down there," she said, "Twice a day."

"What for?" I asked.

"Exercise," a black cat explained. "If you stay fit, and lithe, you'll be chosen quicker to get out of here, so make the most of it, I say, when it's your turn."

I began to think perhaps I should have made friends with the children, but no, there was still the dog even if I could have coped with the children. The stories came over the following days of kittens left in boxes and sacks, half drowned in the river, unwanted Christmas presents, sick cats that cost too much to treat, lost cats who explored too far from home or were stolen and then dumped.

"How long do we stay for?" I asked.

"All different," Maisie said. "Some go in a few days. Like Mac said, pedigrees and young cats first, so long as they are well mannered and not sick in some way. Old cats might never get chosen. Stroppy cats that hiss, spit or claw will be here forever."

Another cat spoke for the first time. "For cats like you, this is a step in the destiny chain. You are young and so far not chosen by your right person, but they will come, I am sure of it, and you will know them when they come, too."

The next day, we were all fed and each in turn, allowed to run, but I was too miserable to eat, and did my best to escape, clawing at the person who tried to put me back in the cage and refusing to keep still when they poked a big black rimmed eye at me saying it was to take my photograph. Whatever they meant, I was keeping it. They'd already taken my independence, my freedom. I wasn't going to let them take anything else.

The tiny space freaked me out. I tried to shut my mind down, Shutting my eyes, sleeping the waking nightmare away, and time passed, the walls pressing in on me whenever I woke, even the run enclosed and claustrophobic. People came, mostly with children, and mostly being led to the kittens whom they then took away. I lay with my back to the visitors, sulking, I suppose. All I wanted, was to go back to the stable and I couldn't understand why I wasn't allowed.

Summer 2010
Time passed, with other cats coming and going. I learned about treachery and violence from human to cat and gained a vocabulary of fury and aggression from cats who, as they were handled, spat growled and hissed from pain or anguish. If people tried to handle me, I lashed out, bit and tore, now afraid that I might end up as some of the other cats had been, abandoned and trapped, half starved before rescue. Maisie went away with an elderly lady who had said she wanted a cat with a similar life span to her own. The cat who told me of destiny became my wisest mentor. "Its time to welcome visitors, Bluebell," she told me. "Your person is coming soon."
I had been in that place so long that I could barely remember what the outside world smelled or looked like and my ability to run or jump was almost gone.
 "How do you know?" I asked.
"I can feel it," she said.
 I wanted to believe her, but was afraid of hope. There had been visitors without

children that I would have gone with if they had picked me, but they had passed me by. I lay now, facing the door, apathetic, my brain in neutral, with nothing for stimulation, just watching the other cats come and go, listening to their tales of horror.

September 2010
At last the day came when the cat sanctuary lady brought in a small lady, who walked quietly as if not wanting to disturb the world, but who looked with eagerness and hope at the cages as she passed, and I knew this was my destiny lady. I sprang to the front of my cage, shouting in my mind, sure she would hear,
"At last you have come for me," and the lady walked onwards to the kittens' room and I sat, in shock, not believing she had passed me by.
 "Wait," said the cat who knew of destiny.
I beat my head furiously against the bars. If only I could get out, make her notice me. I heard the kittens' room door swing open and clink shut with feet echoing lightly, coming nearer...and the ladies returned and stopped by my cage, the sanctuary lady undoing the bolt and opening the door. My destiny lady

was reaching out for me to sniff her hand, and, with certainty, I rubbed and rubbed my cheeks and chin and ears against the out-held hand and she pushed back with affection passing from her to me like an electric current, and a love I had never felt before passed from me to her.

"This one," I heard her say. "This is the one I want." and there was certainty in her voice. She began to withdraw her hand, and I reached out desperately to hold her sleeve with my claw, the sanctuary lady gasping "No," at me, but my destiny lady just laughed quietly and gently disengaged my claws.

"I'm coming back for you," she promised. "They just have to check my house is safe for you, first."

She stepped back and the cage door shut, but I believed her. She would come back.

October 2010

I waited for days. My head tucked in to block out the teasing of a particularly nasty tom who sneered and said "She'll never come back for you. They all say they'll come back, but they don't."

The elderly cat who had told me of the fate

feeling sat up indignantly. "You shut up you silly old thing. You know nothing of destiny and have turned sour in your unhappiness." She turned to me.

"You felt her strongly, didn't you?" she asked me.

I shook my head in agreement and whispered, "I was so sure she had come for me. I felt it from my whiskers to my tail." The elderly cat nodded wisely. "Then she will come. Sometimes it seems humans have to act slowly and write out many many pieces of paper before things can happen. Be patient little Bluebell."

I hated that name, bestowed on me by the cat sanctuary. That was not my name but the elderly cat, whose name was Rosemary, was only being kind so I stifled the desire to spit and swear at the use of such an unpleasant label, glaring instead at the smelly tom with his taunts.

Other people came passed my cage, led first to the kittens and then back along our rows of faces, some desperate, some not caring, others hopeful, destiny doing its thing of joining together those who should be linked to live in happiness one alongside the other. I

had pretty near given up raising my head to look on the day the door finally opened for me. My cage door was unhinged and the cat sanctuary lady reached in to put me in a strange basket, before taking me to a room I had never seen before. A black cat gave me a nod, his greying fur and whiskers showing his age. "You'll be alright now," he said. "I can sense this is the right person for you and you are the right cat for her. Take care though. Remember the song of wisdom."
My basket was lifted into the air, my stomach almost left behind so unexpected was the rising feeling. I braced my feet and tucked myself into a corner for better balance, gazing out of the bars as the world swung and changed around me. The cat sanctuary smells and my friends within the cages were left behind. My nostrils were assailed by the smells of grass and trees, raindrops and farm-scented air. I could hear feet on tarmac and somewhere ahead, the buzz of roaring, growling cars. There was a woosh as a bus went passed and I felt the lady above me's mind spurt with negativity and then be replaced with a shrug and a laugh .
"We just missed the bus", she said. "Well, we might as well walk some of the way as we

have an hour to lose."

The footsteps that had hesitated regained their positive tread. Her feet crunched gravel and then the gait changed as she walked steadily along a road where traffic whizzed by. I could sense her mind, calmness mixed with a thread of satisfied excitement. A steadiness of competence overlaid by contentedness that she had me with her, and through my fear of every strange sound and smell I felt that happiness echoed in my mind and body. I may well cower in the corner with the unfamiliarity surrounding me but I knew all would be well. One of those cars that whooshed past us, suddenly pulled in and a voice called through the open window.

"Would you like a lift? Where are you going?"

My lady ducked her head down to the window level,

"Yes please," she said. "I'm going to Redditch but even the middle of Alvechurch would help."

The car lady laughed.

"I hadn't expected you to be going that far," she said, "But I can drop you in Alvechurch."

I felt my lady drop down into the car and warmth surrounded us as she shut the door with a dull clunk. The engine was quiet and not alarming, the gliding acceleration surprised me and my stomach felt just a little queasy, but my new lady's mind was happy. I stayed quiet and waited. Whatever would I experience next? The car stopped, the engine noise easing to almost nothing and colder air slid around us as we climbed back out to find the trees replaced by buildings, the smells of bread and meat and apples swirling past my nose, alongside the stink of exhaust fumes. We looked into shop windows for a while and then settled into a bus shelter, the lady opened the basket lid a chink and put in a hand to stroke me.

"I'm Margot", she said. "You are coming to live with me. I hope you'll like it. I know everything is a bit scary but it really is OK. We have to wait for a bus and then you are going to ride on a bicycle, which might be a bit frightening, too but it will be alright, I promise."

Her voice was soothing, and the thoughts clear, even if English was something I didn't fully understand, and I was comforted, even if words like bus and bicycle didn't mean much to me. The hand continued to stroke me, sweeping away my fears in its steady gentleness and I became used to the sounds that had alarmed me at first. Then the hand withdrew and I was picked up in the basket as the bus stopped and we climbed on. New smells of dust, grime and so many scents of other people. I sniffed and sniffed, trying to make sense of the odours around me, some ingrained in the seats and others strong from the passengers fidgeting in the seats around us. I held on to the scent of my lady – a mixture of soap, earth, denim, oil and grease, things that I had encountered in the stable, but no scent of horse, or milk, no smell of straw nor saddle leather. I gulped, wondering what my new home would be like. The bus rattled and bounced, swinging around corners that had me sliding around on the towel in my basket. I was glad the bars were keeping me safe inside. Then, with the ding of a bell, we stopped and my lady carried me down the steps and back into the fresh air.

"Nearly home, " she promised. "Just the bicycle to do."

My goodness. The swoop and swing of a bicycle is a feeling all of its own. That first experience was, well, frightening, but exhilarating. The world whizzed by in a wind that blew through the basket swirling the smells of our journey passed my nose at a pace difficult to describe. I've done it many times now and enjoy the kaleidoscope of sights, smells and sounds. A fairground ride for cats. Safe, but taking us to the edge of fear in its unexpectedness and loss of control. The experience ended as we arrived at what I think of now as home, and Margot carried me into a house and up some stairs to a small room with a bed and table to hide under. She opened the basket and lifted me out and seemed happy that I dived under the bed for safety. She simply sat on the floor and read a book, steadily turning the pages. There was food in a saucer and water in a bowl just next to her elbow, but she steadily let the words of the book flow through her mind to mine and only occasionally asked if I was OK. Gradually, I poked my whiskers out, sensing the quietness of the house. No one there but Margot and I. I stretched my nose to the saucer and sniffed. Good food smells curled from plate to nostrils. Edging forwards, I grabbed a nibble and took it back under the bed. There was no retaliation. I snatched another morsel under the bed, and then decided to eat the rest straight from the saucer. Margot continued to read, her eyes sliding down to watch my tongue and furry head but making no move to stroke me. I finished the food and took a lap at the water. Then, with no awareness of danger lurking I decided to explore the room. The door was open and I peeked out, looking at Margot where she sat and read, only her eyes lifting to me occasionally. Was the open door a mistake or was I allowed through it? I peeked out and slipped through the gap. Wow. More rooms. Soft warm carpet beneath my feet, the smell of Margot strongest in the air. Margot didn't move. I padded off to look around, cautiously peering into another bedroom and a bathroom and then down the stairs, ears pricked for movement, but Margot stayed where she was. I half tumbled down the unfamiliar stairs and found another cat standing guard at the front door. How dare it be in my house? I was furious and growled my annoyance. It just gazed into space, totally ignoring me and I heard laughter from the top of the stairs.

"It's not real, Bluebell," Margot said.

I took a sniff at the statue-still cat and had to agree that although it looked cat like, there was no cat scent and it certainly wasn't antagonistic.

"Its a door stop," Margot explained, a smile in her voice.

I gave a sniff of disapproval and checked out the remaining two rooms. Mmmm, nice smelling kitchen. Cosy living room. It looked good to me. I went back to the other bedroom and clambered first on the bed and then the windowsill. It was hard to walk along without knocking into things and a bottle clattered to the floor. I waited for shouting, but none came. To get it over with I went back to the small bedroom and stuck my head around the door.

"Have I been naughty?" I asked in my mind. Margot laughed. "Accidents happen. You didn't mean to knock it off and anyway it's not broken, so its OK," she assured me and I went off, in relief to explore some more, looking out of the window to see what could be seen. Margot came to stand next to me and reached up her hand for a sniff and I rubbed my cheek along her fingers, laying my scent on her, claiming her as my person and feeling the bond of love spread from her to me and back again. I rubbed some more and felt her eager pressure rubbing back. Her eyes crinkled in a smile and she chuckled. "Bluebell," she said thoughtfully, doubtfully.

"You aren't blue. You aren't a bell and you aren't a graceful flower. I can't call you Bluebell. Besides, it's a donkey's name. You're much too fizzy and bubbly to be called Bluebell."

Her eyes widened with inspiration. "Bubble", she said. "Nearly the same but much more like your character. What do you think?" I liked it. How had she known how much I hated my cat sanctuary name? I purred with relief and delight, and she laughed. "Come on then Bubble. Let's get some tea cooking, and I must show you where your litter tray is, too."

We had a weekend to get to know one another well, playing games running up and down the stairs, learning that I mustn't run up the curtains but a glorious game of hiding in the folds and pushing a paw out to catch string was allowed. We laughed a lot and snuggled together in the evenings after a fill of tea, my own food first and a nibble of Margot's to follow as I sat on her lap.

It was a shock when she left me alone to go to "earn pennies" as she put it. A whole day with the house to myself, watching the world from the window and wondering when she would come back to me. At first I was afraid of the big house and being locked in, but it was much bigger than the cage I had spent a year in and I could see out of lots of different windows, seeing other cats in the road below, watching the birds that came close outside the glass, not knowing I was watching them as they fed, and there was food and water left in dishes for me. It was only the not knowing that frightened me so.

It was getting dark when I saw Margot appear on her bicycle, and ran down the stairs to greet her at the door.
"You came back to me," I greeted her joyfully, and rubbed around her ankles with delight and relief. She got my tea and then her tea and we snuggled together in cosy happiness.
"It's your birthday soon," she said to me, and I blinked in surprise, working out something I knew instinctively.
"Yes, it's today," I agreed, certain of the fact but not knowing how I knew.
"Oh," said Margot, picking up my thought. " I didn't exactly know but thought I would make it Halloween so that it was easy to

remember, but maybe that isn't a good date with children out trick or treating and spoiling our celebration so, 24th October is your day. Happy birthday Bubble."

She reached for pencil and paper and spent some time scribbling before giving the paper to me.

"This is your birthday card," she explained. "Look. It's a picture of you."

I gazed at the paper and gave it a sniff, but we don't see things the same as humans and I couldn't make out what she meant. I looked instead into her mind and a picture formed in my head of a brown and black tabby with a white chest, not quite kitten dancing across a room. Me. On the paper she had scribbled on. I rubbed it in appreciation.

Perhaps I should explain that cats are telepathic. Yes, they can miaow and purr, snarl and growl to get attention, or add emphasis, and they can also send messages with body language and whisker vibration but most talking is done mind to mind with cats, and sometimes we find a human that can use the same methods, as I could do with Margot. A specialness to add to our bond of love. A useful skill so that we could communicate with certainty and ease, even books being read coming easily from Margot's mind to mine, and this was a fantastic thing because Margot loves to read, especially books about cats and other animals. How great, I thought, as she read Dick Francis books. How does she know I love horses? Paul Gallico and his cat stories, Bob the street cat, Felix the station cat, Vet stories with cats and horses in them, even detective stories with cats in them and Nanny Ogg's Grebo who I think is my story book hero.

I got used to the pattern of Margot going to work at 6.00am and coming home again somewhere around tea-time smelling of earth and flowers, and a little of trees and leaves, and found I could listen for her mind approaching well before I could see her so that I could run to the door to greet her. Always, she fed me first and then sorted a cooked meal, sitting happily and playing games with me in the evenings, although I have to admit that I love string but never played fetch if she threw things, simply enjoying watching her throw and retrieve until she tired of playing alone for my entertainment. The song of wisdom said that was a dogs' game.

The second weekend, she took me into the garden, where the birds had fed. It felt a big space, the sky so high above us, trees breathing in long sighs and the wind ruffling my fur before heading off to bother somebody else, bringing smells from other gardens in its huffing progress. At first, that huge openness terrified me, with the cloud shadows making patterns that swooped and leapt around me like the snatching glide of a bird of prey, and so many noises I did not understand, but Margot stayed close by, reassuring me and I crept from my hiding place to explore my own garden smells, discovering the scents of other cats who had taken this garden as their own. I bristled.. "My garden," I thought. "Mine alone."

After two days of safely exploring every nook and cranny, I felt the desire to see what made the other scents the wind had brought to me. I gazed at the fence and reckoned I could climb it. Taking a dashing leap, I got my front paws on the top and scrabbled with my back legs until my tiny claws caught the splintering wood and I levered myself up. I gazed down at another garden and launched myself forward to land clumsily on the grass. It smelt strongly of a male cat, and looking up, I saw him, white with black patches gazing out of the long glass windows of the house. A lady came to stand next to him, and I felt vulnerable, turning to rescale the fence and clamber back to the safety of Margot. She seemed happy I was back, too, my first independent adventure over safely. We scurried back indoors leaving the excitement in the garden.....but …...now I was curious. How many other gardens were there? How many other cats? And were they friendly or foes to vanquish from my territory.

The next adventure came with Margot that evening. The sun was shining when she got home from work.

"Come on," she said. "Let me show you more of outside,"

It was to become a routine for the rest of our lives – the morning walk almost every day and at first, this evening walk in the sun. Those first walks were around our block of houses, showing me the safe places with no roads, but instead footpaths and verges, even a big field to run and dance in. At first, I was so unfit from my time within a cage that I could only manage 100 metres before flopping onto my side for a rest . There were children playing on the paths who cried out "Oh look a kitten," and ran towards me so that I ran into the hedge and hid. Margot explained to the children that I was very nervous and if they wanted to stroke me they would have to be very quiet and still. They tried but I wouldn't come out, remembering those hands that held me tight and hurt me. I met them several times, but they could never quite keep still enough to earn my trust and we only got to know each other from a distance.

Did you know that humans can take their fur off? That first month, I stuck to Margot like a shadow as much as I could, not even wanting her to shut me out of the bathroom, so I was amazed when she made water fall from the ceiling, took her fur off and got all wet in the water, even adding strong smells to her underneath skin, and then washing them all off again. It made me laugh and laugh. What a funny way to wash. She told me she had to do it like that because her tongue wasn't big enough to wash her whole body with and she washed her fur in a box of sloshing water that hummed and growled, hanging it up afterwards to drip and drip and drip to get dry while she wore different fur. It takes a lot longer to get ready to go out what with deciding which fur to put on, but I suppose it has advantages when some days are warm, and others cold. My coat takes a bit more time to adapt to that.

November 2010
Gradually my muscles grew strong and I began to trot and then run and I could sense

Margot's apprehension every time I disappeared under a parked car, not knowing where I would come out and I loved to tease her, hiding behind hedges, telling her to wait while I leaped a fence and explored a garden she said was not hers and couldn't enter. Sometimes I reappeared three or four houses down the road, calling out, "Hahaha. I'm right down here. Come on Margot Margot" so that Margot would jog to catch me up as I ran eagerly onwards.

My territory seemed vast, no cats to bother me except that white and black cat next door. I had hissed a warning at him through the glass and he had shut his eyes in a smile and laughed.

"I'm Bill," he greeted me. "I was great friends with Monster who lived in your house before you. I'll be happy to be your friend too."

At first, I could only go out beyond the garden with Margot, because I hadn't learned my name, nor how to use a cat flap. Just once, in the morning before work, I had leapt the garden fence and set off to explore, not returning when called and when I did return, Margot was gone and although I could get into the conservatory, the house door was shut. I sat, forlorn and lost, my nose pressed against the glass, waiting for her return, meowing hopefully, but no one came.

It was lunch time when she hurried into the living room, looking hopefully towards where I sat. I put my paws on the glass and patted it urgently. She sped across the room, as relieved as me when she opened the door and hugged me tight. I hugged her back and snuggled my head under her chin.

"I have to get back to work," she said, " so stay in now and I'll see you later."

I was delighted to be able to curl on the bed, safe and warm. From now on, if Margot called, I was going to come immediately, I promised myself.

There was a week of terrifying bangs and whistles that had me cowering under the bed, in the bathroom or under the table. Bright lights flashed across the skies, the cat instincts making me run from hiding place to hiding place while Margot tried to explain the house was safe, that it was only fireworks and I had no need to be afraid but I could not over-ride my instincts and the fear was strong. It was wonderful when the nights returned to peace, with nothing worse than the bang of a front door, or a car engine murmuring past our house.

We went to the vets in November. It was time for my vaccinations. I struggled hard against Margot's attempts to put me in the basket, thinking I was being taken back to the sanctuary, but we cycled a different way, different houses and smells, more cars on busier roads to shy away from within my basket. The door of the building we arrived at went Ping, as it opened and a lady greeted us with a smile that lit her whole body. I sensed Margot's happiness in greeting her.

"I have a new friend," she said, a touch of sadness in her voice, but also laughter and excitement. She lifted my basket for the lady to see, and she greeted me with warm fingers, the scent calming.

"She's not the brightest of cats. Not smart, like Monster was," Margot said, an image of me growling at the door stop strong in her mind, "but she's fun."

"I'm sure she'll learn with you," the lady said. She turned to me.

"I'm Auntie Tracey, your nurse," she explained. I went also to meet Richard, my doctor who hurt me a little with a needle and checked my teeth and ears, running gentle hands over my coat as he spoke to me and Margot, and I knew he meant me no harm. Then we went home and had chicken because, Margot said, I had behaved so well.

December 2010

The next big adventure, with so much to learn was at Christmas. First, my house went sparkly with glittering strings festooned from lampshades and curtains and Margot took a plastic tree out of a box especially so that I could play hiding and hunting in the box, with plenty of scratchy noises, string and holes to poke my paws through, or peep through before I leapt and play-killed the knotted ends that had wriggled tantalisingly just out of my reach. I love that box which I play in specially every Christmas time.

I had another adventure to come. The basket I had arrived in appeared and I was full of fear, terrified I was being taken back to the cat sanctuary, even though the last journey had not ended that way, when I was lifted into the basket. What had I done wrong that I was being taken from my destiny home? But Margot didn't put me on her bicycle, as I had expected. Instead she gathered up a big bag and slung it on her back. Carrying another bag on her wrist, she hugged my basket tight and we walked up the hill and down the other side where a rumbling monster came growling and roaring, its weight and size making the very air and ground tremble. "Its a train," Margot told me as I cowered back in the basket, wanting to run away and hide elsewhere, " And even though it makes so much noise it can't hurt you in your nice safe basket. It is taking us to our holiday house and my mum and dad. Don't worry. I won't leave you. You're safe." I wasn't so sure. Trapped in the basket, I could easily be forgotten and left behind.

So many noises. The beep beep-beep and rumble of closing doors, the revving of engines and then the sensation of movement whilst trees and fields and houses and other buildings flashed into view and away again. Sometimes the rattling stopped and the scenery stood still and the doors beeped and rumbled and beeped and rumbled again,the space we had had almost to ourselves gradually filling with other people, tired and yawning or plugged into wires, their faces blank and listening to the scratchy noises in their ears. Just when it looked as though no more people could fit in, Margot buckled my basket lid closed and stood up and I was afraid she would leave me and mewed loudly. "Don't forget me. Don't leave me here." Margot gathered me up as the train slowed and stopped.

"I won't leave you, I promise," she whispered as she carried me at her side and we half stepped, half jumped off the train and then found a quiet place to sit, I covered in a blanket over my basket to let me stay hidden amongst the bustling feet and the rattling wheeled suitcases. It seemed an age before we moved again, down an escalator that made Margot glide magically and then another roaring monster appeared and we climbed within it. This monster had a quieter roar, even though it was bigger, and there were more people chatting and moving about inside it. I watched with cats' curiosity. Learning and learning as best I could. Why did the people come and go each time the train stopped? Where did the smells of bacon and egg come from and where did they go as people passed us with the train still giving that sense of motion while we stayed still and the scenery fled away behind us. Margot opened the basket lid but I was happy to stay where I was, on the table, the world within view whilst I could hide away if I wanted. We stopped and changed trains twice more, my nose sniffing the smells of fields and station, dogs, food, people, and trains. Noises clanged and echoed, passing us by as we crouched unnoticed in our untroubled corners.

"We're almost there," Margot told me at one point. "One more stop and then it's our station and then we can walk into Yeovil and catch a bus. OK?"

The words were soothing and I felt happy to trust my destiny lady. I was tired but content. The train stopped and we climbed off, joining a hundred feet tramping over a bridge, up a hill, across a road and then gradually spreading out to all go different ways. Our way was the best. Smells of tossing turbulent water, reeds and wet grass, animals I could not imagine the shape of and the white stuff that surrounded us - snow. I came eagerly forwards to press my nose to the basket bars

and smell these new, amazing smells. I felt the basket tip me forwards but didn't care. Margot chuckled and we stopped on a snow cleared rock for a while so that I could sort out the different scents and match them to what I could see: waving reed heads, ducks, willow trees and a swirling river rippling and spinning with a music of its own, a song of centuries, timeless and power-filled.
"Better get on or we will miss the bus", Margot said and picked me up in the basket again. "We'll come back this way. You'll see it again."

I liked the bus. I could sense the happiness of the passengers chatting to the driver and the other passengers, the driver greeting people by name. There was some kind of excitement in the air that swirled each time the bus doors opened and closed to let a new passenger on or one of the chatting crowd off. "Have a good Christmas," they called as they left. Margot seemed just a little uncertain, restless, urging the driver on in her mind, wanting to be somewhere we had not yet reached and I wondered why when the people around us were happy.

"Almost there," she whispered to me as we

swung into a village street. The bus stopped and we got off, me still afraid I would be left behind and mewing as a reminder from behind the bars.

"Just a tiny walk now," Margot promised, "although its a bit slidey. We'll have to go carefully."

We walked slowly. Occasionally there was a jerking slide and regain of balance. Now the smells were of car exhaust, woodsmoke and mud under that overlay of snow. We left the main street with its busy cars and scurrying people and turned into a quieter road where Margot paused. "Gosh, It's an ice rink," she said in her mind. We went more slowly and then stopped again. Margot put the basket down and I was afraid I was going to be abandoned. She took off the rucksack and carried it a little way in her hand, put it down and came back for me, and did the same again and again, breathing nervously, afraid of the ice with the unusual, uneven weights to carry.

At last, we turned off the road and climbed some steps and then there were people greeting us at a door and warmth and more smells of cooking and Margot set my basket

down and opened the lid so that I could raise my head and peep out while she took off her coat and hung it up, then lifted me out. Another lady crouched near me and said, "Hello Bubble",
and I knew instinctively, this was another safe person I could trust. I rubbed around her legs in greeting.
A rumbley voiced man appeared at a door and also greeted me but, you know, I'm never quite trusting of those rumbley voiced people with their extra strength and height and I couldn't quite bring myself to rub his legs, circling close but not quite touching and then I gazed around me at a long thin room that seemed to turn corners with doors open wide and more rooms to explore. I set off to see what this new place was like while Margot and Mum followed at a distance to see what I would do. This was a big place with rooms that joined one to another in a circuit that I could go round and round in, with other rooms going off in other directions. Margot and Mum left me to explore and sat in the kitchen, having showed me where my litter tray would be and my food and water bowls set. I loved that I could go round and round, appearing from either door to the kitchen to

give Mum and Margot a surprise and then trot off again on another circuit.

"She hasn't learned about cat flaps and doesn't come if I call so we'll keep her in this visit," I heard Margot say, but the words were irrelevant as I continued my exploration. The man, I learned, was Dad and he was following me, laughing quietly as I poked my nose into cupboards, crackling papers, inhaling dust along with the mustiness of unused clothes. I found Margot's rucksack next to a bed along with my basket and the litter tray, and tested out the bed we would sleep on. Mm soft blankets welcomed my furry feet and tickled my nose. It seemed good to me. I kneaded it gently liking the woolliness between my pads. My stomach was now settled and hungry after that long long journey and I was ready to eat from my familiar reassuring bowl. Margot was eating and chatting to Mum, the atmosphere harmonic, and then we all moved to a small lounge where there were so many many shelves to climb on, Margot jumping each time I stepped delicately between the ornaments and sparkling decorations, Mum laughing at her nervousness., as I was, too.

With every reachable shelf clambered upon, I checked out the laps, settling, after several walks between the three, on Margot and curled up to sleep. I loved this house. Margot rarely left me for long and sat around for hours with me on her lap, or exploring close by as she chatted. On the second day, there was a great unwrapping of parcels set around a tiny tree, even cat treats for me. I was so overwhelmed that I had to go and lie quietly in our bedroom while more presents were unwrapped. I had never been given presents before and had not expected the lump of emotion that filled my throat. For the first time I felt part of a family, sharing their laughter and smiles, being one of them.....and I had no gift to offer in exchange which made me sad because I wanted to show my love and gratitude in return. I slipped back into the room as the aroma of coffee replaced the rustling of wrapping paper and then had the excitement of sharing lunch. Was that sumptuous food really all for me? Yes. It was.

Mum and Margot had been going next door to water the plants for a neighbour who was away and leaving me behind. I so wanted to go with them that the next day, when Mum opened the front door, I stepped out, hoping Mum would come next door with me. Mum seemed to hold her breath, with a frisson of worry and didn't come outside. I walked about, enjoying leaving my tiny exquisite paw prints in the snow, feeling the flakes, now ice encrusted, crunch under my pads as I stepped delicately. The coldness was a new sensation which began as interesting but became a gnaw of encroaching pain so I stepped back in through the open door and Mum gave a relieved chuckle as I padded back down the hall to see if Margot was awake. I leapt on the bed and put my cold paw against her cheek, purring as her body heat warmed my freezing pads. She was just waking up – what perfect timing.

" Your paw is freezing!" Margot exclaimed as she sat up and rubbed her cheek. "Where have you been?"

Mum chuckled again from the hall, overhearing our conversation.
"She slipped out of the front door while I was getting the milk in, made a few snow pictures with her paw prints, sniffed around a bit and came back in, good as gold."

Margot looked at me half angry, half laughing. "I thought we said you were staying in this holiday," she admonished, "but no harm done as you came straight back in, I guess."

The morning passed with me doing my best to slip into the one room I wasn't allowed in – the snooker room. It smelled of polish and wood and appeared to have a big table to play under, but every time I sneaked that way, the door was shut and I was brought back to the main room.

Mum and Dad had a television, which Margot did not At home, we listened to the radio instead. I discovered an armchair strategically placed in which I could laze on my side and watch the moving pictures, with music and voices adding to my enjoyment. I listened to the words and tried to join them to the pictures, adding to my vocabulary as best I could. What a way to learn! If I was spotted in the armchair, I was removed as sitting on soft chairs was not allowed for cats in this house, even though Margot allowed it in our house. I thought this a silly rule and did my best to break it at every opportunity, just to show that nothing terrible happened if I sat in a chair, so long as kept my claws sheathed and cleaned regularly of course. Once, Mum placed a vase of flowers between me and the television, but luckily Margot sensed my displeasure at this inconvenience, as I tried to peer round them, moving them over and explaining to Mum why she was doing this. "Bubble can't see the TV", she said. "The flowers are in the way," and I knew I had won the battle of cats on chairs.

That afternoon, I sneaked into the snooker room and found Dad in there, dusting the table. I walked under the table, approving of its height, the dangling table cover and its huge expanse, perfect for a game of hide and seek chase. I slipped out on the far side and looked out through the glass floor to ceiling window.

"Do you want to go out?" Dad asked. There seemed to be a great deal for a small cat to explore out there, and no obvious dangers so I ran to him excitedly and with a giggle, he flicked a handle and slid the glass back, letting in a breeze carrying the smell of snow, mud and grass and leaving a gap just big enough for me. Gratefully, I slipped through and trotted off to explore. My goodness, what a huge outside there was. I sat with a bump in the snow, gazing at a vast expanse of untouched whiteness leading to a hedge, the branches weighed down by yet more snow. I could pick up the scent of Margot's shoes and followed it round to the back door, but the door was shut and I had no idea how to get it open. Not worried I returned to where I had left the house, but that door was also shut with no Dad in sight. The milk door would be open, I thought, and hurried around the house, but that was shut too. I hurried around the whole house again, hunting for a way in or a way to tell Margot where I was but no one saw me and no door would open when I pushed. I sat down on the door step and cleaned my paws thoughtfully. I had seen no sign of Margot through the windows. Perhaps she had gone to that other house that I had wanted to visit. I followed her scent around the boundary hedge and up to the front door but that was firmly shut, too. Now I was getting cold and it was getting dark. A bat swooped over my head, making me jump, and I wondered if small cats were prey to any other sky dwellers that might swoop down and snatch me up. My aloneness suddenly filled me with alarm, a black panic engulfing me. Where could I hide? I scampered around the house and found a shed door ajar. Squeezing in, I leapt onto a bench, away from the cold floor, and miserably sat down on a piece of sacking. How silly I had been to leave the house alone, without my Margot to keep me safe. Hadn't she told me I wasn't to go outside this holiday? Now I had no food, no people to keep me safe and nowhere to keep warm. There were people shouting somewhere along the road but I didn't know what they were shouting about. I curled into a ball for warmth and tried to sleep. Someone was making scraping noises in the distance. Metal against stone, scrunching and shushing and then the plop of thrown snow. If only Margot could find me, I thought. I'd never go out without permission again – or at least not out of sight. I'd be back in the door in a flash if I saw it closing with me on the outside. I dozed and shivered, trying to think what I should do, and time passed, the darkness deepening into midwinter dusk. Snow icicles dangled from the roof and across the only window in my shelter. Would I freeze in the dark dark shed?......and then I heard the gate opening to this back garden, where I was hidden, and Margot's voice shouted loudly, "Bubble, Bubble where are you?" I leapt to my feet and squeaked as loudly as I could "EEE_EEE_OW WWWW". Footsteps paused. "Where are you, Bubble?" Margot's voice again. I repeated my cry, my voice

sounding too quiet to be heard beyond the shed walls, but I was doing the best I could.
"Bubble? Call again," Margot said and she was just the other side of the wall I lay by.
"EEEEEEOWWWW," I called, desperate to make her hear, and the shed door was pushed wider, and there was Margot. I leapt towards her squeaking with joy and Margot ran to pick me up, putting my cold body inside her anorak to warm it and cuddling me close.
 "Bubble ……...Bubble…..Don't ever go off like that again."
Her voice was quavery with expended tears and present rejoicing as she took us back to the safe warm house next door.
 "I found her," she called joyfully as she closed the back door behind us, and looking up at her face, I saw the drying tear stains and the stress lines fading and felt emotions wash over me.
 "She really cared I had gone," I thought. "She loves me as I love her. I must not make her sad that way ever again."

One of the only bad things at Mum and Dad's house was that Margot lost all sense of time – late up for breakfast so that I had to ask Mum to feed me a snack to keep me going, and worse still, late to bed, staying up well past our bed time, talking to Dad or watching a film when I was ready to curl up on her feet and sleep. Even when I pointedly leapt from her lap and sat in the doorway, ready to lead her to the bathroom, and then went back to pull at her leg she continued to chat. A claw to the elbow and rolling on my back to nibble her hand at last brought the response I needed, an apologetic "Bubble says its past our bedtime. We normally go to bed at 9 at home. I'm over an hour late," and she said goodnight to Dad and followed me to our room at last. In her mind, she explained that Mum got up early and went to bed early, and Dad got up late and went to bed late so to talk to both, she had to have less time in bed and I decided to give her just an extra hour before insisting on bed at night.

As the holiday past, I was as good as a curious kitten could be. In the evenings, I sat on Margot's lap while all three of my new family placed plastic tiles on a flat board and talked in numbers and odd words, moving the tiles round in a concentrated way on a small rack and rattling the tiles around in a bag. It made Dad mutter and groan and Mum and

Margot laugh although I didn't really know why. Margot let me come to visit the house next door. It had a smell of male cat but no cat appeared. I wondered what he was like and what he would think of my exploration of his home. The days passed, and I learned a new game my family played – ping pong. I could sit under a table while, taking it in turns, my family stood each end of the table, grasping small bats and sent a tiny ball skimming across the table, backwards and forwards, ping- pong it said as it bounced and hit a bat and ponged again on the table above my head, their feet dancing, giggles and shouts of glee and frustration and the ball landing on the floor, spinning away for me to watch, and chase if I wanted. I loved that game and was overjoyed each time they played.

I wondered if this was the new pattern of our lives, but it seems holidays are only short interludes. After ten days, Margot repacked her rucksack, leaving presents behind and taking others home and we had another journey, my curiosity over-riding my fear so that I demanded the right to get down from my seat and explore the carriage.

"Well, only a little way," Margot said, and I remembered the promise I had made and just peeped around the seats we shared, gazing at the children opposite who cried out, "Oh look, a cat. Can we stroke her, please?" Margot said I was a bit nervous of strangers so only a little bit and one at a time and very gently, and I found that with Margot to protect me, the children were not as frightening and violent as I had expected. In fact, it was quite a pleasant experience. Their mother smiled gratefully, glad of the distraction on their own long journey. We changed trains three times and I became more used to the array of sounds that battered my ears. Tannoy announcements, the crash and clatter of so many types of wheels, from trains through porters' trolleys to suitcases, bicycles and push chairs. There was the woosh and bubbling gush of the coffee machine, voices everywhere and of course the honks and roar of the trains with the odd whistle thrown into the mix. Margot mostly took me into waiting rooms or to the far end of platforms so that I could sort the noises and, with her explanation of what they were and how trains can't leave their tracks, I became calmer and more confident. The warmth of the trains themselves made me sleepy so that the journeys passed in a dream, the changes of scenery magical each time we ascended and descended. How did the land move each time we climbed into our box like carriage and why did the trains come gliding into the station with so many people getting out that I never saw get in?

I was tired when we arrived home. We ate quickly and then slept peacefully, glad to be secure in the home that was ours.

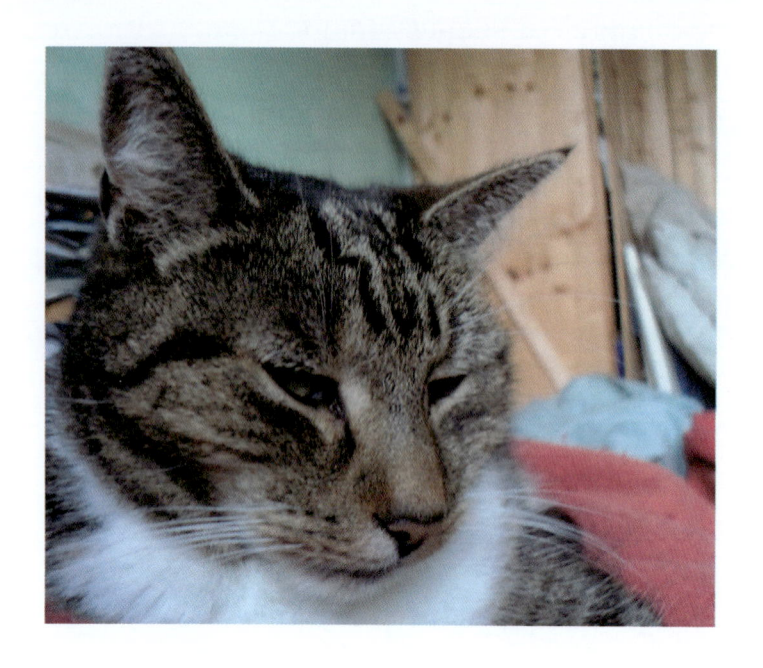

January 2011.

After that, I had to learn how to go in and out through my very own cat flap. I have heard other cats say that you should always get your human to open doors for a cat, but I liked my independence. For the first time, I could go to a midnight cat meeting or hunt under a full moon when only the noises of the night could be heard and the human world slept. As a newcomer, and an almost kitten, I was expected, at meetings to observe and learn while the older established cats discussed things important to cats. I sat in awe, ears pricked, and was especially attracted to a tabby, more black than brown, his chest broad, with powerful shoulders but slim hips and an amused glint to his eyes. He noticed me watching him and gave me a smile all of my own. At the end of the meeting he came to me.

"I am Rupert," he said, his voice accented, "and your name is..?"

"Bubble" I replied.

"Hmmm, he said doubtfully. "I think you may call me Beau and I will call you Belle, for we are both beautiful, are we not? Belle is also short for Bubble, I think."

I felt my heart stir with excitement and twitched my whiskers in agreement.

"Where is your home?" he asked and I led him to my house. We sat outside and I told him of my holiday, the trains and buses and the scents of the river.

"So, you are an experienced traveller," he said admiringly. "I too have travelled, by train and ferry across the seas, and of course, in cars too."

"Have you been on a bicycle?" I asked curiously.

Rupert looked at me with uncertainty.

I smiled secretively. "I'll show you some time," I promised.

He nodded. "The dawn is not so far away. It is time we slept. I will see you around ma Belle. Au revoir."

He sauntered off and I slipped through my two cat flaps – porch and front door to tuck myself in for a couple of hours sleep on Margot's feet.

March 2011

There was a day when Margot said, "I'm going for a whole day's bike ride, Bubble, so I'll be late home, but I'll be back in about sixteen hours just late for bedtime, after it's got dark." and then she took her bike and left. She left me extra food and water, but I didn't know why, hadn't understood the words or the image in my mind. Tea time came, but no Margot. Other people got out of cars and went into houses and the sun went down behind the trees. The moon shone instead, and stars twinkled in the darkness.

"Margot has got lost," I thought. "I'd better go to look for her."

At first, I hovered in the road I knew, afraid to go further but still she did not come, so warily I set out along the road she had cycled away on, creeping stealthily from hedge to gate, to wall, listening and sniffing for danger. I was a long way from home, wondering how far I dared to go, when I heard the clicking of a free wheeling bicycle, and with relief picked up Margot's tired but happy mind. I darted out from the shadows as she came into sight and she braked and stopped. "Bubble, what are you doing right down here?" she asked.

"I came to look for you," I spoke in my mind.

"I told you I'd be late back," Margot expostulated.

I wriggled, shy and embarrassed and said, "I know, you said, but I didn't understand."

"Oh Bubble, I love you," she said.

We walked home together, both a little wiser in our relationship, and Margot put the pictures in my mind. A train ride to the mountains, disembarking at a tiny deserted station and an adventure cycling along a river, through towns and villages, scenery rugged, the water turbulent, and I loved the sharing of the story in her mind.

April 2011

Hunting is a learning experience. Yes, I see you raising your eyebrows in surprise. Based on instinct, it is true, and added to through the song of wisdom, but it takes the flapping of a pigeon's wings nearly breaking one's nose as you leap from ambush to grab their tail, or the angry dive bombing by a young crow's parents as it hops enticingly and invitingly along the ground to teach one that some birds are just too big for a small sized cat. Margot said she didn't want me catching birds and it served me right, as I mewed for rescue from my hiding place and the crows cawed their supremacy from the branches above my head. She even poured a bottle of water over my head when I forgot and caught a young sparrow that hopped right in front of my nose as I lay in the shadows of a conifer tree. I released it in surprise and it flew away unharmed

It seemed Margot rarely hunted. And wanting to help her learn, as she taught me, I brought her mice to practice on, banging loudly through the cat flap and yelling " Mowus" to alert her as I thudded up the stairs, the mouse held gently in my jaws. I have to say, Margot was a quick learner in snatching the proffered mouse before it gained its wits and ran. Sometimes the most quick witted mice got away and we had a merry midnight chase up and down the stairs and in and out of rooms and cupboards, but I could never get her to give that killing blow and then the mouse would disappear while I was distracted so that in the end I had to snatch the mouse back and take it outside before it got lost in Margot's hands.

And what of Rupert? You may wonder. For several months, we spent many free hours together, hunting as a team, he telling me of a far away country called France where the food and hunting was better and the sun warmed a cat all year round. I thought I was in love, and then I saw him with another girl. Two timing me! How dare he! And that was the end of that.

At about the same time, two new cats arrived in my road. Charlie, the same age as me, and tabby, and Molly, a cheeky young white cat with just the tips of her ears tinted black and a black saddle spot on her back. We found it fun to play chase, racing around the houses and through the gardens, and then Charlie found if he ran at other cats, they would turn tail and run and he could chase them, too. I found it worked for me, as well and another game was born. "Ha Ha Ha" I would think as the cat fled and I sped after it. To be honest, I could never quite keep up. That long stay in a cage had lost me a year in muscle development. In a way it made the chase more fun. What would I have done if I caught them? I have not a single idea.

At home, I was learning about Margot's hobbies, many of which I could share, like reading books, drawing, knitting and sewing. As the nights had grown colder, I loved reading best, tucked on Margot's lap, our bodies providing a shared luxurious warmth, the words flowing from her mind to mine so that I learned of things far beyond the world I was part of and if I felt she had read enough, I had only to lie across the pages or poke my nose up from underneath the book and she would put the story down to rub my chin and cheeks, and perhaps fetch us some supper.

One afternoon, I was flummoxed by her attention in fitting bits of cardboard together, all different shapes and colours, rattling them around in a box and trying the bits all over the place, her absorption excluding me when I wanted to play. I went to ask Bill, the white and black cat next door who knew so much and was so calm and placid that the world felt safe whenever I was with him, what it was all about and what I should do.
"Oh. That sounds like a jigsaw puzzle," he said as we sat close, Bill on his shed roof and me on the fence. "All you have to do is lie on the pieces on the table and start cleaning, or, if you prefer, you can sit in the box. Both ways, Margot will be looking at you and after

trying to work round you will probably give up and talk to you instead."

"Thanks, Bill, " I said and returned home,where I confidently leapt from chair to table and, sprawling elegantly across the growing pattern of joined together pieces, began to clean in a business like manner "Oh Bubble! Excuse me, I'm trying to do that bit." Margot tried to pick me up but I rolled to cover more bits, delighted, managing even to push some bits onto the floor. "Ha, ha ha," I laughed inside.

"Bubble!" Margot cried indignantly, trying to lift me up again, but I batted her away with my paw, enjoying the game. Margot laughed. "OK. I get to put in four more pieces and then I play with you," she offered.

I considered and decided to agree, rolling sideways but watching suspiciously in case she forgot her promise.....and yes, cats can count in case you were wondering, at least as far as is necessary for a cat. I let her put in five pieces before pushing up to her hand and rubbing hard as if I just couldn't manage without her stroking me for one second longer, and she looked sheepish and turned her full attention to me for a good while. I saw her eyes stray longingly back to the laid out pieces and decided to sit and watch, just giving the odd piece a helpful poke with my paw when she appeared to be stuck and getting a grin for my efforts. I decided jigsaw puzzles were quite good fun. Acceptable entertainment for cats as well as humans, especially when I realised the full picture was of cats!

May 2011

I was just completing an early morning walk with Margot when I saw the white pedigree cat from down the road crossing to examine a neighbours bushes. The "run at the cat and chase game" was still a favourite and I bounced away from Margot to chase my chosen victim. Much to my shock she didn't turn and run and I had to stop abruptly, unsure what to do, and feeling just a little silly. She gave me a slow inspection from ears to tail and back again, looking me straight in the eyes, her nose raised in disdain.

"We female cats have too much dignity to play such silly games," she said in a haughty tone. "Especially cats from that house."
She indicated my home. "I will show you," she announced decisively.
I sat back on my haunches in surprise. "What do you mean?" I asked.
"It's alright for silly boys to run about practising their machismo, but we have more subtle means of control, and far too much grace and elegance."
I glanced back at my house.
"Yes, but what about my house?" I asked.

Her eyes were clouded with sadness for a moment and then her head came up with defiant pride.
" Before you came, there was a cat of such immense power that he led this neighbourhood for eight years, right from when he moved in until he died, despite a terrible accident where he had to learn to walk again with only three legs. Even in his last weeks he stood up to the bully cat that tried to do as you just did to me and vanquished him with a curse and a look. He fought only on his first day and from then on

ruled by word and thought, teaching us to live peacefully together as we had never lived before."

Her head came up with more pride and she pushed down on some strong and rising emotion. "I was his lady. We were so in love. I so beautiful and he so handsome....although the accident took away his gloss and litheness, he was still beautiful inside." She turned to gaze at me and hold my stare. "So. That is your inheritance, little cat, and Bubble is not the name of a top queen, so I shall name you Alexandria as your name to rule and, as I will soon be getting old and ready to join Monster perhaps in a few years' time I will teach you how to take over my role as leader."

I looked back into those beautiful blue eyes, studied her long white fur and arrogant poise and gulped. How could I learn that confidence, that arrogance, that grace?

"Gosh," I said.

"My name is Lily," she said. "I have heard you swear and curse and shock the toms attracted to you, but who you consider beneath you. That is the foundation we will build on. Where did you learn such language?"

"At the cat sanctuary where I lived almost a year," I told her. "Cats came in angry and frightened and ready to fight anyone who touched them and they swore and cursed and I couldn't help but notice how well it worked."

She nodded approval.

"I will meet you tonight once you have seen your human tucked into bed and asleep and the teaching will begin. Goodbye for now, your human is waiting for you."

I raced back to Margot who was standing by our front door, watching, amused that Lily had stood up to my headlong dash, and I reckoned she knew what had been said. I entered the house with a new set of emotions. I was living in the house of a King. I ran up the stairs and looked out of the windows at the place I might, someday, rule, noting how of all the houses I had the best view of my domain. No doubt Monster had used his observation posts to always know what was going on in an apparently magical way. I would do the same.

Summer 2011

Time passed and I shadowed Lily as she marched the neighbourhood, dishing out a word of praise here and an admonishment there, factual rather than emotional, I saw the other cats gave her respect, never sassing her, always listening and grateful for her praise. She was tiny in size but even the biggest toms bowed their heads to her confident rule. I tried to do the same and it worked with all but Charlie and Molly. Charlie just still wanted to play, and I have to admit I still wanted to play, too when I was with him, our speed and agility so evenly matched we never knew who would win our games, both of us normally ending in falling down helpless laughter. Molly was miffed. "Why should Lily choose you and not me?" She complained. "I'm better than you at jumping and climbing. Your tabby looks are so-o common. I'm not doing what you tell me, so there."

She was enraging. Sassing me when I made a comment. Walking insolently across my conservatory roof with hard footed paws, and sitting right in the middle of my garden daring me to chase her. Of course, I did, and she would run, but she laughed and smirked as she ran, knowing she had made me act in an undignified manner. It was upsetting.

Margot told me just to ignore her and she would give up, but that was hard to do. She got so much in my face.

Charlie was getting into trouble for being too aggressive, humans stepping in to warn him off when he chased their cats, even though he meant it only as a game.

"I can't help that I'm growing big," he said, mournfully licking off the water someone had just sprayed over him with a hose pipe to stop him chasing their cat. With my new leadership knowledge, I nodded agreement but said, "Maybe it's time to just play chase with cats who want to play. You are becoming quite handsome. There'll be girls who want to flirt with you. Chase them, but maybe only when their humans aren't watching because they might not understand the game."

Charlie considered. "It won't be as much fun, but I think you are probably right," he sighed.

I never got to know if my suggestion worked because both Charlie's human and Molly's (Thank goodness) moved soon after that and for a while, I felt quite lonely despite my learning with Lily, who was now leaving some of the day to day inspections with me. We had organised our road's cats into a look out team, always some cat on duty, ready to deter or report invaders. The early morning brigade could be a bit sloppy and needed a good bit of growling before I knocked them into shape. I learned to laugh internally at the youngsters who had forgotten their role and slipped off post to inspect something they had never seen before. I was often out walking with Margot at this time and would see them dashing back to their posts, pretending they had been there all the time. I would pretend I hadn't seen unless it became a habit when a sharp reprimand was required and then they would be almost standing smartly to attention the next time I inspected their patch. It worked well and meant I knew straight away if new cats came onto our territory and could go and have a word about cat meetings, the rules on no fighting and of course joining the team and respecting each cat's space. There were two new cats moved into the house next to Charlie's where there had only been dogs before. Bud was a growing lad with enormous paws and an extra toe which made him the most amazing tree and fence climber. He was besotted by me and would wait to show off his latest trick, mooning about on the pavement outside my house. He would be so busy watching for my reaction that he often fell off branches and his attempts to sprint across the grass at full speed, shouting "Watch this," as he tried to catch, maybe a pigeon meant he failed to catch any of his intended prey. His house mate was an older female called Verona. We got on well, her accepting my leadership but me never feeling the need to impose any rules on her because of her steady, tolerant nature, rolling her eyes and laughing at Bud's attempts to impress. "Boys!" we would laugh as Bud sidled off to hide his embarrassment, and yet he never learned and always had another scheme planned to demonstrate to me whenever I passed.

Secretly, I was impressed by his way of scaling trees with his wide stretched paws. I have never quite learned how tree climbing is done. Perhaps because my claws seem to lack length and strength. Perhaps it goes with my brown tabby mottled colouring that allows me to blend in to the fallen leaves on the ground but not those growing fresh and green up in the canopies. I am designed to be a ground hunter, and my goodness, I am good at it when I try.

In my first Summer with Margot, we went

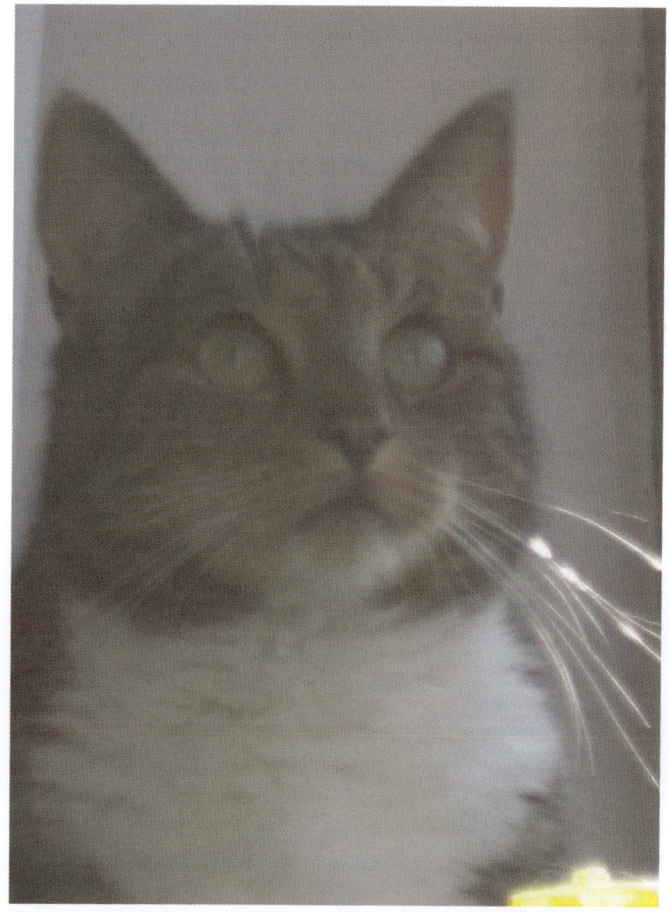

back to Mum and Dad's house in Somerset, the train journey hot and long, but with experience, I was less afraid and more interested, pleased that I had learned the buzzer meant shutting doors and that the scenery would soon begin to flow backwards passed our window. I realised that children on trains love cats and will want to look at me even if they don't touch and they always think of me as beautiful. I had been learning too from sitting close on Margot's lap when she read books, listening to the pictures in her mind and the words on the page as they flowed behind her eyes. My vocabulary improved so that I could make jokes about being Margot's secatary when she wrote on bits of paper or I ran to answer the phone and listened to messages when she was out. We chuckled together over my help with the acats (accounts) when she added up her earnings from her job as a gardener.

We laughed together when a book said there was a pause in the proceedings and I put my own paws forwards to cover the page. I liked best, the books with cats or horses in them, and learned new ideas from the cat who got Paul Gallico to write a manual for stray cats and kittens. Of course, my mother had told us much of what she said in the song of wisdom, but maybe I had slept through some of the song or maybe I was taken away before the song was complete. I tried out some of my new knowledge with Margot, but as she had also read the book, I learned she had to be happy to do as it suggested, failing therefore to convert my food to smoked salmon and caviare – not that I minded. I love chicken and ham and bacon best– she had already grasped that I should be allowed a smidgeon of any food she ate and if I liked it, she would give me more.

There was advice on vets and how to enthral humans by being cute and sweet – a thing that became almost an obsession with me as I sought ways of being cute and sweet, Margot laughing affectionately as I asked. "Am I cute and sweet?"

"You are," she would say, rubbing my head …..but I was never sure if she meant it.

Dick Francis books reminded me of my kitten home, the horses watching us benignly and indulgently as we played amongst the plate like hooves and listened as the horses spoke of races run, the heady feeling of leading the pack, the speed and recklessness over fences, the overwhelming instinct to win. Felix the station cat opened my eyes and gave me more understanding of those monsters we had travelled within. I heard how Felix was not afraid of people and had so many friends and I decided that I, who had always fled from strangers, might, with caution, try greeting the people who passed my home. I saw, through the picture words passed from Margot's thoughts to mine, how often we cats bring comfort and joy and laughter to our humans. Just as Marvel would say, Margot's happiness depended on me. Anyway, I have digressed.......

Mum and Dad's in the Summer was different to my Winter visit. No inside tree covered in shining lights, no glittering, sparkling string and no presents but now I could use a cat flap and understood there were times when I should come if Margot called my name, I was allowed outside. There was a field we could walk round where no other humans went but our family, and I could run down it at immense speed, paws reaching for the sky as I leapt. There were bushes to hide in and mice and voles to hunt. Badgers had dug holes in the grass for me to use as a toilet – most considerate. The space was huge! A cat came from next door and was greeted by Mum as Marvel. I growled, wanting this place as my own, but Margot told me Marvel was nice and kind and really we were the intruders on his ground. He was polite and inviting but I felt surly and grumpy and wouldn't let my guard down, so he went away saying he would come back later in his light hearted way. On the second morning, I sat on the steps between split level gardens, my ears and nose pointed forwards, concentrating hard on the scents and sounds of this amazing place. Mum and Margot were in the house, I think keeping an eye on me but not interfering in my independent exploration. I was not aware of the black tom that crept up from behind me until he was within touching distance and then he said "Boo!". I turned my head and leapt into the air with a shriek at his swarthy scratched face and fur torn muscular frame so close to my rump. So tough did he look with his ruffian's smile that I ran without thinking up the steps away from Margot's protection when I should have run to the cat flap. Ears back and flat, I could sense the Tom chasing me as we rounded the house corner, sprinted down steps and spun around another corner, his black paw nearly touching my tail. The front door was tight shut as we sped on and I swerved another corner, almost back to where we had begun, but this time Margot was out and calling from the cat flapped back door and the black cat slipped away as I ran to safety, his telepathic chuckle echoing in my mind. "I'll see you later," he called.

Margot was stroking me and calming me as I re lived what had happened, and gradually realised if he had wanted to harm me, he easily could have done. It had been a game, like Charlie's and perhaps I did not really need to be afraid despite his ragged looks. We spent the afternoon in the paddock, me snoozing in the bushes, an ear pricked now for danger, Margot making a racket, trimming back the hedges that surrounded our garden and raking up the droppings before calling me in for tea time. It seemed this was what Margot did every Summer – came to cut the hedges, play with me and walk under the hunters' night sky with me before bed. Once she was asleep, I went nervously when Marvel called, inviting me to their cat meeting. News of my coming had got around and the meeting, dominated by farmyard toms, smelt of testosterone and tom cat spray. It was hard to make out their words, almost another language to the cats of the Midlands where I lived and the tom cats were more savage and coarse in their vocabulary. They looked at me openly assessing my ability to breed strong kittens and moved sexily, rippling strong muscles to impress me. It seemed, though that Marvel, with his quick mind and lightly muscled body was the leader, taking charge of the meeting, and asking me to tell them of where I lived and how I had travelled on trains and buses to get there.

"Weren't you afraid of being trapped in a basket?" one tom asked.

"No," I replied. "I was, last visit, but then I saw Margot was using it to keep me safe and although I don't like getting into it and having the lid shut, I'm not afraid of the basket itself. I mean, once we are settled on the train, Margot lifts the lid and I choose to stay in and be safe when I could get out of I wanted."

The tom scratched an ear thoughtfully. "I'd ha been gone soon as buckles undone," he said, "But then maybe not if your Margot feeds you well and gives you good shelter and warmth."

"Oh yes, she does," I agreed.

We chatted on, comparing my street and house life to their farmyard existence, both interested and keen to absorb more knowledge. The meeting ended as the moon dipped, and Marvel escorted me home to my cat flap.

"Most of the guys are OK. But mind out for Jaggy. He can't help it but he is sex mad. He'll hang around a bit. I'll try to warn him off and keep an eye out for you."

"Thanks, Marvel," I said happily, glad that I had overcome my nervousness and gone with him to the meeting.

I slipped onto the bed, listening to Margot's regular breathing, watching, with love the expressions crossing her face and tucked myself into a ball on her feet while I had a couple of hours sleep before breakfast time, my dreams filled with farmyard toms and the hunting of mice.

Jaggy was a bit of a pest, appearing out of shrubs and hanging around the cat flap. At first, I tried to be polite and evasive, but when he nearly landed on my back, I let lose with my cursing and swearing. He sat back, shocked and then backed away. I was amazed at the effectiveness of the curses I had learned as he slunk off and never returned. Whatever had I said?

Margot and Mum decided I was comfortable enough with my surroundings and they went out for a whole day, leaving me in charge of the whole house and garden. I felt proud that they thought I could manage, patrolling the house and eventually slipping up to the paddock where I would see when the car returned. High on the hill, I felt safe as I watched the world beneath me. Marvel padded out from the hedge and sat a little away, giving me space, not crowding me.
 "It's special here," he told me. "A crossing of the old ways. I expect you can sense that."

Now he had said it, I could. A flowing of energy beneath the land, and I had instinctively sat where the powers that flowed gave positive energy and took away the energies that harm. Marvel sat quietly – company but not intrusion, calm and sure of himself. After a while he commented. "You and I are linked in our colouring. Your lady said we are difficult to tell apart, me just having a little more white to my cheeks, our markings the same, but also we both share a house with one person so that we are equal, both of us giving and receiving love and care. Even when they seem strong they need our love and support, Bubble. Did you know that before you came, Margot brought Monster.? What fun we had, chasing each other about once he was recovered from the journey, and he and I were alike in our leadership. We were good friends while he visited, and Margot's heart was almost broken when he moved on, so I know she needs your love to heal."

"What was Monster like?" I asked curiously.

Marvel cleaned a paw, thoughtfully. "The best leader I ever met. Calm, sure, confident, quick to laugh, gentle in correcting others, and...." his stripes crinkled into a laughing smile, "always able to get his own way, the charmer. Stubborn and determined. He never gave in to anything, I suspect. Not even losing a leg."

I sighed. "I wish I had met him," I said. "I am to take over his leadership. It is decided, but I am no great thinker. I have no confidence. How will I do it?"

Marvel blinked as he thought. "Your knowledge of weakness is a strength. Just don't try to bluff. When you aren't sure, ask for advice and others will respect you more. You'll be confident once experience comes. You'll see". He got up. "Bye now. Time for tea." and he was gone as my family came up the hill in the car, returned from their outing.

I returned to Redditch, wiser and already more confident thanks to Marvel's words and the admiration of his friends, those tough old farm cats, and the respect was coming. As new cats came into our road, I became busy, greeting them, explaining the set up, and with no toms old enough to lead, they all turned to me, with Lily happy to gradually pass her mantel on.

Autumn 2011

With Margot, I had a new game. Adding names to my title, which seemed to add to my queenly status, and somehow she picked up on my thoughts as the names came – Alexandria, she knew, even though it was

Lily's name for me. Then we added Esmerelda from the Terry Pratchett books and Victoria – the top witch and the stately queen. We had read of Madam Shang Kai Shek, which sounded a good exhibition name, but when Margot explained about cat shows with small cages, arrogant cats and lots of strangers staring at you, I decided the name would remain unused. I would not demean myself by attending exhibitions even if I might win.. Much later in life, I added Hekunikiti which I heard listening to a radio gardening programme, with its internal cat reference and couldn't resist Mauritius – with Mum picking up the Maurishepuss phonetics. I think that's enough titles even for a cat as queenly as me. Don't you?

2011 to March 2014

For two and a half years, after that our pattern was the same, Margot going off gardening, day to day while I looked after the house, accepting phone messages in my role as secatary, and letting Margot replay them when she got home.
"She said that to me before," I confirmed,

listening to a customer asking us to ring her back, - the exact words she had said that afternoon when Margot was out working.

One Winter, Margot was busy in the living room. Together, we cut the wall out of a cupboard under the stairs, put four paving slabs in a square, and made a wall out of pretty coloured bricks. Then a van delivered a big black metal box and some tubes, I was fascinated. What was Margot doing?

"It's a wood burner," she told me.

A man came and made a lot of noise while Margot sat with me in the bedroom, He left a big hole in the wall. Margot seemed pleased, but I couldn't think why. It made the room colder. The next day the man came back and put the tubes together through the hole and that night we had our first wood burner fire. I was frightened when Margot made fire with a little stick, but then the room became warm, and Margot and I sat and watched the flickering of the flames. It's mesmerising, beautiful and magical.

The next day, I ran excitedly to the box, saying, "Do the warm, Margot. Do the warm," and Margot did. From then on, Margot has brought home wood from her customers' gardens, and I have helped her cut it all into logs,so that every Winter we can enjoy a relaxed sprawl on the settee with the flames flickering and heat emanating through our whole house. I feel such a lucky cat to have such a thing.

Once a year, I had to visit my doctor for a vaccination. I didn't really think it necessary as I was perfectly fit, but the basket would come out and I knew it was that day. Once, I managed to slip out of the front door and sat on the corner of our drive, waiting, When Margot tried to grab me, I sprinted along the pavement to the next corner, where I looked back to see Margot running after me.

"Catch me," I called telepathically, and ran to the next corner. Here I almost let Margot catch me, her fingers brushing my tail so that I spun on my back and rolled away before sprinting down the back alley behind our gardens, Margot close behind. We spun around the next corner, and then the next with me screaming inside with laughter. "Ha ha ha".
I passed our front door and started a second circuit, Margot still running and calling for

me to stop. Half way round the next circuit, I jumped a fence, and vanished, listening to Margot running by and calling as she hunted for me under cars and in the hedges, but I was well hidden until I was sure the appointment was cancelled. Margot gave me a half angry grin when I turned up, and having rebooked was more careful to have me trapped inside the house for the next appointment when I made a half hearted attempt to hide behind the piano, knowing she would catch me in the end, but the chase game is great fun.

There were two holidays at Mum and Dad's each year. One summer, I met a fox in the garden there. So glossy and athletic, his red coat shining in the sun so that I sat with a bump in the vegetable patch where I had been exploring with Margot close by. "Aren't you supposed to be afraid of foxes?" she asked me, but all I could murmur in my mesmerised state was : "He's beautiful."
The fox was busy and paid us no attention, disappearing through the hedge to the farmland beyond. I went, the next day to the same spot, hopeful of another sighting, but he didn't come again. I have seen foxes near my

home since then and always, my heart hammers with excitement at their perfect beauty. Should I be afraid? I truly do not know.

Sometimes Margot would leave me alone and in charge for a whole week to go on a holiday without me. I hated that, afraid of the empty house. I worried she might never come back as other cats in the sanctuary had told me happened. I felt so alone on the bed at night with no sound of breath, and no warmth from the feet tucked beneath me. She did her best to explain what was happening before she left, leaving me alone at home with a lady coming to feed me but even with Margot touching my paws and ears for every night away, I found the waiting hard, not wanting to eat, listening and watching for her return, and scratching the lady who fed me when she tried to offer comfort. It was Margot I wanted, and nobody else and I fretted and worried that she might not come back to me.

I have heard of cats that refuse to talk to their people after they have gone away for a week, but when Margot came home, late at night, tired and ready to share our bed, I turned my back only for a second before running to her, shouting, mind to mind, "I'm so glad you are back," and I knew Margot was equally glad to be back with me. We ate together and snuggled close for the rest of the night, glad to return to our old routine. Each giving a sigh of happiness to be together again. She told me of her holidays. Learning to ski, seeing the Northern Lights and snow covered lakes and mountains, the stars bright, too many to count, the night time snow glistening, tobogganing down mountains and looking at reindeer, the pictures strong in her mind so that I knew what she had seen and what she had felt and shared the excitement and exhilaration of her adventures.

March 2014
In 2014 Dad died and Margot hugged me tight and cried. Then she pushed her emotions into a box in her mind and in a daze, set about contacting customers cancelling appointments and booking a train ticket to Mum's for the next day. I didn't really understand what had happened until we got to South Petherton and, although I looked everywhere, I couldn't find Dad. Perhaps I should have mentioned before that

Dad and I had a teasing relationship. He slopped around in a red hat and clumpy boots that seemed to warn of danger to me. Sometimes he crawled around pretending to be a big dog to frighten me and only gradually did I see his underlying softness and gentleness and a simple desire to be loved. He wore trousers that felt smooth and uncomfortably silky, but we had some great games in a house with sliding glass doors where I could go out of my cat flap and ask to be let in through another door, and Dad and I loved that game, with me running straight from door back to cat flap and going to another door where Dad, laughing, would let me in. I missed him. The house was quieter without his clumping boots and stomping stride. Margot spent hours talking to the telephone, which sometimes upset her. I was there, sitting on her lap, ready to walk with her in the dusk and dawn when the orange sun seemed to give her strength. It was Margot's birthday while we there and an astonishing number of people came to celebrate, sitting chatting on the settee and in armchairs. At first, I hid in the hall, peeping through the distorted glass doors, but Margot seemed relaxed, sitting on a sag bag, chatting so I crept nearer, and eventually joined in. Marvel's lady was there, but Marvel had also died and she watched me sadly. I couldn't help stir memories of her previous happiness. I wish I could have given comfort, but her grief was still raw. On the last day, Mum said to take me to Jennifer for her to say hello and maybe give just a little comfort in her loneliness. We did that and then Margot called me to go home, but I wanted to explore Jennifer's garden and trace the places Marvel had been and I refused to come. After all, it was another hour until the bus would go – I was used to that rhythm from eight visits before. I slipped into the hedge and hid in the shadows chuckling to myself as Margot tried to find me. She gave up, and went into the house and I went to explore Marvel's territory and pay homage to that wise, steady cat. Margot came back out and called again, "Bubble, Bubble", but I stayed hidden. I still had time to explore.

It was strange that Margot didn't come to call me when I expected. I waited for the double call "Bubble, Bubble" but there was nothing. I went uncertainly to the house and in at my cat flap. Mum was in the lounge.

"Margot had to go, " she told me. "You're staying with me for the week. Keeping me company," she added.
I wasn't sure what she meant and went to find Margot – it was time to go. The bedroom was empty, except for my litter tray and basket. No Margot and no rucksack. Mum had

followed me.
 "She had to get an earlier train to get back to work, " she told me. "She's coming back in a week my love."

I understood her words, but how could they be true? Margot and I were never apart. I searched the house and garden, refusing to accept my mistake in not coming when called, thinking I was being clever, forgetting the promise I had made to myself to always come when called. I was furious with myself, and somehow also furious with Mum for letting Margot not find me when it was time to go. I went back to our bedroom, to be near Margot's smell and felt sadness swallow me whole. It was as if the blackest rain cloud hovered over my head and my throat ached with loneliness. Mum gathered me up to comfort me but I wriggled furiously free, enraged by my helplessness to put right what had gone wrong. Margot needed my comfort and I had let her go alone. I couldn't eat that day, just curled on the bed willing the week to hurry by. I heard Mum talking on the telephone that evening. "I think Bubble thinks it's all my fault," I heard her say. For three days I hunted every day for Margot, checking the hedges and all round the flower beds, every room in the house, over and over again, waiting at the top of the steps for Margot's return. A van drew up and a man and a lady got out, but not Margot. They went into the house and made lots of noise, banging about in the roof space. I peeked in, seeing boxes and boxes stacked in the hall.

Now what was happening? I sat in the shrubs in case I was put in a box, too, and watched the man and lady pack the boxes into the van. They left and I slipped in to find Mum, deciding to sit with her for a while, sensing her sadness.

The next day, Mum was busy making up beds, but Margot's stayed as it was. Mum seemed to be overlaying emotions of sadness and excitement with practicality as I watched her work, going off to the shops to bring home more supplies of food. Perhaps Margot was coming back, and some other people, too. A car came up the drive and I ran to greet it. It must be Margot, I thought, but it wasn't. A lady almost the same size as Margot and a boy got out and Mum came to greet them. They hugged each other and then carried bags into the house, me watching from a distance, still hoping Margot would also appear from the car. The new people were noisy and energetic, bustling about and not interested in me. The hope I had held was smothered, my loneliness and grief stronger than before. I felt excluded by the chatter., ignored even by Mum who had tried to comfort me before. "Margot, Margot," I called in my head. "Please come back. I love you. I need you. I feel so lonely".

Two more days slipped by. I stayed mostly outside, the noise too much for my aching heart. Curled round for comfort I sat in the paddock, missing Margot, missing Marvel, missing Dad. All the people came out of the house and got in the car, but I stayed where I was, absorbing the sun's rays. After a long time, the car came back and I heard doors opening and shutting but couldn't be bothered to raise my head. And then I heard a voice, "Bubble, Bubble."

It sounded like Margot. I raised my head. Was I dreaming? The voice came again, "Bubble, Bubble," and I scrambled to my feet and ran, helter skelter back down the paddock.

"Wait for me, wait for me. I'm coming. Don't leave me again."

My inner voice shrieked in time with my racing heart as I almost fell down the steps in my haste. Where was she? I tumbled through the cat flap and found the place full of moving feet. Too many feet. Too much noise. I turned and ran out again and the door opened behind me as I scurried across the patio and the voice called again with urgency, "Bubble!" I stopped. It really was Margot's voice. I turned, and there she was, coming towards me. "Bubble," she said again and I ran to her outstretched hands and let her gather me up and cuddle me in her arms and against her chest, my head tucked under her chin and I purred and purred as she held me as if never wanting to let me go again, and I hooked a gentle claw into her sweatshirt, hanging on tight, not to lose my Margot again.

It seemed there were things to do. I sat on Margot's lap or followed her close behind and slept on whichever bed she slept in while people came and went, papers were rustled and written on and there came a day that felt different. Everyone was subdued, uncertain, dressed in strange clothes and after breakfast, they disappeared for a while. It seemed they were going to see Dad off at his funeral. Cats don't do this, so I didn't really understand. Margot smelled of mints which she said made it difficult to cry and offered them to the people who I know now were her sister and nephew. They came back later, their minds numb, their thinking slow and wary, drinking tea, concentrating only on the present moment, and were surprised by a knock on the door. Relatives had missed the funeral but found the house. There was more bed swapping as they stayed the night. I just aimed to be there, giving comfort to Margot as she stroked and stroked my fur. There were more phone calls and then some sorting of Dad's belongings. Margot's sister and nephew would be staying when we left to help Mum sort things out and we would be returning again in three weeks. This time, I went in the basket with no struggle as we raced to catch the train from Taunton, where I had never been – a different station, a train that stopped less often and went more smoothly and faster. I was learning more and more about the world. Margot went around in a state of numbness, needing my comforting warmth. Part of her mind was surprised that things went on as normal, with Dad gone. She acted on a sort of auto pilot, part of her mind shut off with thoughts she couldn't think yet hidden away. I stayed close when she was home, knowing she needed my proximity.

May 2014
We went back to South Petherton again and this time it was Sue and Braith that left first,

the garage now empty of cars and dad's bicycle gone. Fewer smells of engine and oil. The bed cleared in the snooker room. Little changes that meant a lot. Margot worked hard in the garden, tidying, weeding pruning, letting her grief go in physical exertion, crying in the darkness under the stars as we walked after sunset. …..and then we were home again with life almost back to normal.

Two Christmases followed with no Dad, a few tears and a determination to celebrate differently, but cheerfully, and then Margot was busy in Redditch cycling out with her camera and when we went again to South Petherton for Mum's birthday, Margot took the photos and it seemed Mum might come to Redditch to live. Time passed, Margot busy in the Summer with her gardening work, home with me, or enjoying that one week's holiday in the Winter. Then Mum came to stay and there was panic as Margot tidied the house for her visit. It all seemed a bit of a rush but at the end, Margot said, "Mum's coming to live here. We'll be selling your holiday home but you'll be seeing Mum up here instead in her new house. So we won't have to keep going on the train every year".

I was a little disappointed as I now felt an experienced traveller, no longer afraid of those roaring monsters tied to their tracks, knowledgeable about whistles and tannoys and the scurrying feet rushing to travel to who knew where, and I loved that paddock with the hill I could run down and the rooms in their circle. I would miss them and Dad who had lived there.

2016
Margot was excited. Mum was coming to her new house and Margot was going to meet the removals men to get the furniture sorted before Mum came on the train. It was Autumn, the leaves changing colour and falling crisp and crackling to the floor in the golden sunshine. I wondered what the new house would be like.

Our routine changed after that, with Margot spending Saturdays with Mum, and me busy managing our road, Lily content to watch from her windows or her front step. I was confident now that Margot would always return, not so worried when she said she was going to Ireland for a holiday and would be learning to ride a horse while she was there. I

grinned up at her as she explained, and stood up. "I can show you," I said eagerly, spreading my paws wide and waggling my tail for balance. "You ride like this."
"But I haven't got a tail," Margot smiled.

My smile wavered, and then I giggled. "Then," I said mock seriously, "You will fall off. Ha ha, ha ha." Margot laughed too. "Maybe I'll try a different way," she said.

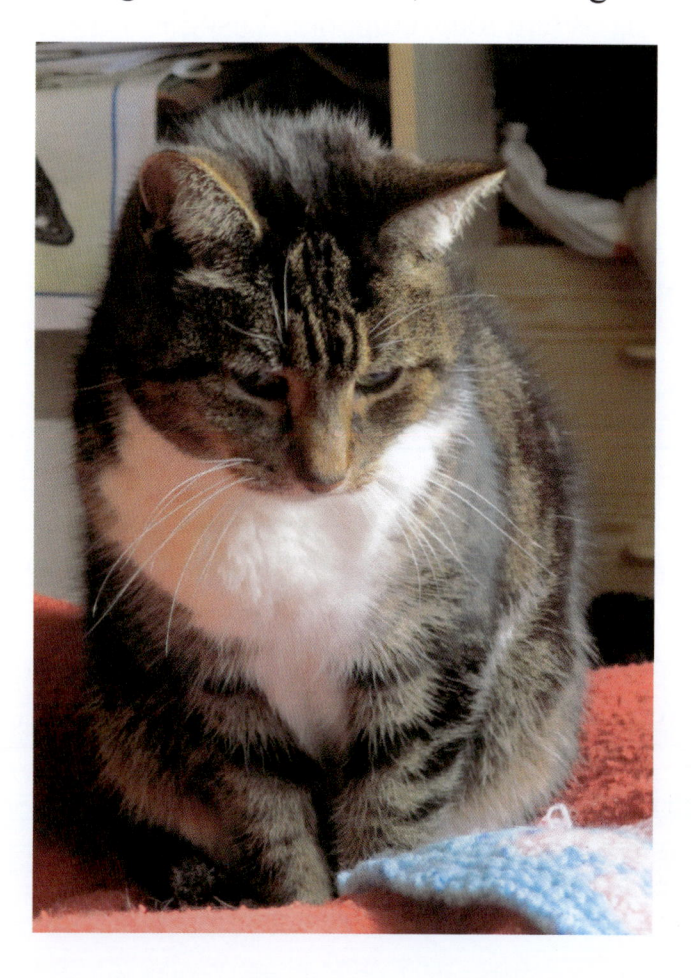

She came back from that holiday, released and smiling and told me of adventures on trains and ferries that were late, getting lost in Dublin, and again amongst the hills and mountains, cycling in circles. She told of the horse that knew what to do, and riding on the sand, the sea roaring, gale sized waves breaking beneath the cliffs, and I was glad for her happiness.

Do you remember me telling you how frightened I was of the fireworks that banged and whistled and flashed? There was anther thing that frightened me. A black snake that sometimes seemed to get in Margot's mouth and made horrible squeaks and rumbling noises. When that happened I used to run outside and wait for the noises to stop before creeping back in to see if Margot was OK. Well, both those fears were cured together. I must tell you first, that I understand about music. Margot and I would listen to the radio in the mornings and evenings, and I enjoyed the voices chatting to us from inside the little box and the music they made, but then Margot played me some saxophone music played by someone called Julian Smith, and I just felt my whole mind and body relax, and then Margot made the black snake make the same music so that I realised it was tamed. I crept up to listen and loved the music just as much, and then, Margot played the saxophone music on the nights of bangs and flashes, and I found I didn't mind those outside noises any more. Some years, after that, she played other music and you know, that worked just as well.

2020
More time passed, and then the world changed. It began just before a Christmas when Margot felt ill and then Mum was ill with a bad cough that was hard to cure. Margot, being a gardener had time to be home and laze around as she got better, with less work to do in the darker months and I was glad I could snuggle up to keep her warm and comforted. Then, it seemed the whole world was ill and people were dying everywhere. Margot had got better and started working hard and then the radio spoke to her and said people were to stay home, if they could work from home, to stop spreading an infection that was killing hundreds of people, and the world went quiet. No aeroplanes nor whirlybird helicopters in the sky. No cars dashing here and there. Only the radio's constant chatter and the voices of neighbours over the fence on one side and a silent house on the other. Margot stayed home for a whole week, the sun shining hot so that we sat in the garden most of the time, under the cherry tree's shadow, and Margot brought out her

computer and started to type, with me tapping the odd key when it seemed she needed help, reminding her about meal times when she seemed to have forgotten and calming her when she seemed distressed. I listened to the words she typed and realised she was writing a book which began as a true story of how she began to garden at a Tudor house, and I was in the story. The words said my Margot went back in time without me and she told how much she loved me and wanted to be with me and even though I knew it was a story, with Margot tapping the keys beside me, my heart ached for the Margot in the story and the story Bubble who had lost her Margot, lost in the past, and I knew that the feelings were real. Margot wrote fast, the story flying from her fingers, almost done in a week, and then she went back to gardening, while most of the world stayed home in fear. She seemed often frustrated and angry and I learned she was saying things through the telephone to the radio so that thousands of people heard what she said about the illness called co-vid that killed so many, and I was proud of her as she fought to talk sense and stop the people dying. Later in the year, she hugged me and told me I was famous because our book was published and I was in the story, and the radio talked to us through "zoom" so I was famous again when the radio lady saw me on Margot's lap and asked about me. The cats heard on their radios and were quite amazed at my fame.,

Another Summer of Margot gardening followed, the pattern steady and regular, our lives a kind of harmony, even though it seemed co-vid hadn't gone away and people kept their distance, one from another and many it seemed worked from their houses instead of going where they went before so that, if I lay outside my front door, I met more people passing by, and the next Winter, I was given more fame in a book of poetry Margot published with photos including me looking quite sweet, cute and pretty, too, I think, and another story followed, with me helping as best I could., even though I wasn't in that one.

2022

Lily died the next year, and joined Monster – another sky cat amongst the clouds. I was now truly in charge. Louis had taken her place in the house down the road, a pedigree kitten with all the looks but none of the arrogance and brains normal to his breed. We were good friends, with me explaining how Lily had taught me and the importance of the house he lived in. I had other friends and many admirers. From being mostly female cats, our road had turned into a road of neutered toms who fought for my attention. As a leader, I refused to romance with any of them, but chatted often to Louis, even though he was a bit lacking in courage, allowing other cats to enter his garden so that I had to see them off for him whilst he hid in the house, amazed at my courage. Milo , who lived two houses away also become a good friend, acknowledging my leadership, but not afraid to chat as an equal in knowledge and experience, and I welcomed his thoughts.

Margot was home just a little more in the covid year with less going off to sail her boat, and for a while, no visiting Mum so often and I enjoyed our time together. She seemed angry with the world more often, feeling frustrated and helpless. Mum gave her a book called the Dalai Lama's cat. We read it together, with me comparing my knowledge with that of the Dalai Lama's cat, who wrote that story. At first, I knew so much more, but sitting on the Dalai Lama's lap, or in the office of the monks, she began to learn as I had done, through listening and observation and she passed her learning to us in three books. Margot was fighting hard for three things from 2020 – co-vid year onwards, the end of unnecessary co-vid deaths, the saving of the planet from climate change, her anguish at what we are doing to the planet spilling out in shouting rage at the radio, her thoughts on the children and the animals and plants that would die if we don't start taking positive steps.

I think she is right for even in my tiny world, the seasons are changing and I see less bees, less of the butterflies that used to dance above my head , fewer beetles, even less birds. Three hot Summers with no rain and plants dying, then 2 years of rain, rain and rain, with failed nestings and insects dying with no food for them to eat as they hatch from eggs or transform from chrysalis or larvae to eventually reach their adult form. Finally, there was a local thing called "Save the library" which I didn't understand but seemed to take hours of Margot's time, writing e-mails and having meetings, reading newspapers and writing letters. The Dalai Lama's books seemed to change her life force. Less anger and more positive efforts, even standing to be a councillor, which took her away from me to put bits of paper through people's doors, and chat on their doorsteps of the things she cared about for a day or so each month. I guess I was glad when the phone call came. "You didn't get in, but you were very close," the phone voice told her. "OK" Margot said, calmly. "On to plan B, then."

Summer 2024

There were fleas everywhere and Margot hadn't been able to give me my drops because I might have had to be microchipped where the flea drops go, on my neck. I was itchy and could feel them crawling all over me so that I couldn't sleep and pulled my fur out to get at the horrible creatures. Margot kept vacuuming and spraying, moving me from room to room, washing the blankets and sheets every day and hardly spending any time with me because of all the cleaning. I sat outside as much as I could, getting thin and looking shamefully scraggy with my fur all scuffed up, and the rain making me look bedraggled and uncared for, even though Margot was furious about the microchip and what it had done to let the fleas get everywhere. The drops didn't seem to be working, even though they were what my doctor gives us. People noticed, and someone called the RSPCA. Two people came while I was snoozing, and I thought they were cat napping me as they took pictures and tried to read my new and hated microchip. I struggled and yelled and the neighbours came to protect me and explain why I was so scraggy while I hid under the neighbours' car. I was terrified and found I could no longer relax outside our house unless Margot was there, and even then I hid under vans and cars when I could. My life was miserable.

Margot sat outside with me, or in the hall if it was raining and eventually she got rid of those fleas by using other sprays and washing the carpets in rosemary and lavender. People had started feeding me extra food, which I suppose I needed because of all the extra washing I was doing to get rid of the fleas, but even with the extra food, I didn't seem to be getting back to my normal weight so I had to go to my new doctors, who seemed frightened of me and even when I only looked to see what the lady doctor was doing, she backed across the room saying I was going to bite her. Margot was angry and took me home again, feeding me more and more food, even trying different sorts to help me get fatter. Then I had to go back for tests, and that made me hungry and then sleepy and crying out for Margot as I sat in a cage. I was so happy when she came for me, but why had she left me there for so long? Had I done something wrong? I wasn't sure, and that worried me.

My eye sight was blurring. I started to follow people, to ask them which way was home, and one night found I had been taken into a house I couldn't get out of until, Margot came looking for me and I was taken home, then someone I didn't know picked me up took me back to the vets and I slept alone in a cage, crying in my loneliness until Margot rescued me the next morning, and said I had best live indoors except for our morning walks.

Autumn 2024

I am getting tired now. My joints ache and the battle against fleas last Summer was exhausting intermingled with the inputting of that microchip which was stressful and uncomfortable. Last year, I was strong enough to take on the dogs that encroached on my territory, banishing them with my direct walking to the other pavement, but this Winter I just want to curl up in the warmth and be with Margot as my eyesight fails and my legs ache when walking. Each moment seems precious, no second must be wasted as my life ticks away.

Winter 2024

Margot said, in the Summer, that the conservatory was falling down and my goodness, she was right. Glass windows were slipping through rotten frames and the door became crooked and couldn't be shut. Its been stimulating, amusing and interesting to watch Margot work with drills and hammers and saws, building a new framework and taking out windows to put in new frames with a fair bit of muttering and cursing, frustration strong in her voice at her lack of strength and height and the stickiness of the builder's sealant that made dismantling so much harder. I sat and gave encouragement, examined drills, and did my best to make the work more entertaining without delaying progress too much.

I love our new conservatory with fewer draughts, less smell of dampness and decay and a warm seat on the settee. It has been good to do this project together as I think it might be the last. I have so wanted Margot home with me as I reach my final year. I no longer want to be independent but to not waste any more time apart. Thank goodness Margot is a gardener and can be with me through much of the Winter days, me curled on her lap or close against her legs. Love and friendship given and received. Comfort shared.

Christmas has come and gone. I've needed help from the doctor to enjoy that special day. We went to Mum's house, with so many of the rooms lost and the garden not so big either. I enjoyed snuggling on the chair, Mum and Margot close by, chatting and the television on. There were presents to give and receive with crinkling paper and warm laps to sit on – a happy day.

And so, here I am nearing the end of my life, tucked at my Margot's side as she taps the keys to put down my thoughts, her face creasing with tears, trying to swallow the grief. She smiles and tells me I am still cute and sweet, that she will love me forever, and I tuck in close, The wood burner has been lit and my blanket gives me extra comfort and warmth in the Winter half light of a cloudy day. We've had great times together, only this last year of decline and chaos making a dent in the happiness and I know it is time to be released from the pain in my gut, my failing eyesight and my stiff old limbs, Who knows what comes next? Will I begin again as a mewing kitten or in some other form, and, in the Buddhist way, perhaps meet again with Margot, two lives to be entwined together forever, or will I become a sky cat controlling the clouds and the rain as Margot thinks Monster did for many years while he waited for Lily to join him, riding the wind and exploring the heavens. He was a colossus amongst cats, so confident and determined, knowing his path in full. I have tried, as Lily taught me to follow in his ways, leading the other cats, making decisions and keeping order as best I can from this special house at the centre of all, and now I have passed all that to another leader, Jace, who came here just a year ago but understands how to lead through earned respect and I can rest. Its been a good life. I sense Margot's frustration that maybe she could have saved me this last year from fleas and disruption but that path of destiny cannot be altered. The song of wisdom tells us this is so, I hope she will soon remember the laughter we shared for over 14 years and put the sadness of parting aside. Goodbyes are hard for her, I know. I wish I could make it easier for her with a final tease – maybe a walk across the keyboard and an eloquent operation of the mouse. Maybe, when she moves to add a log to the flames, I will pinch her warm seat.

I hope you have enjoyed the story I so wanted Margot to write and perhaps you will remember my words as you consider sharing your life with a cat. We are, of course all different, but what we all share is that need for independence (despite our desire for human company) that I hope you will love and respect when you share your home with your destiny cat.

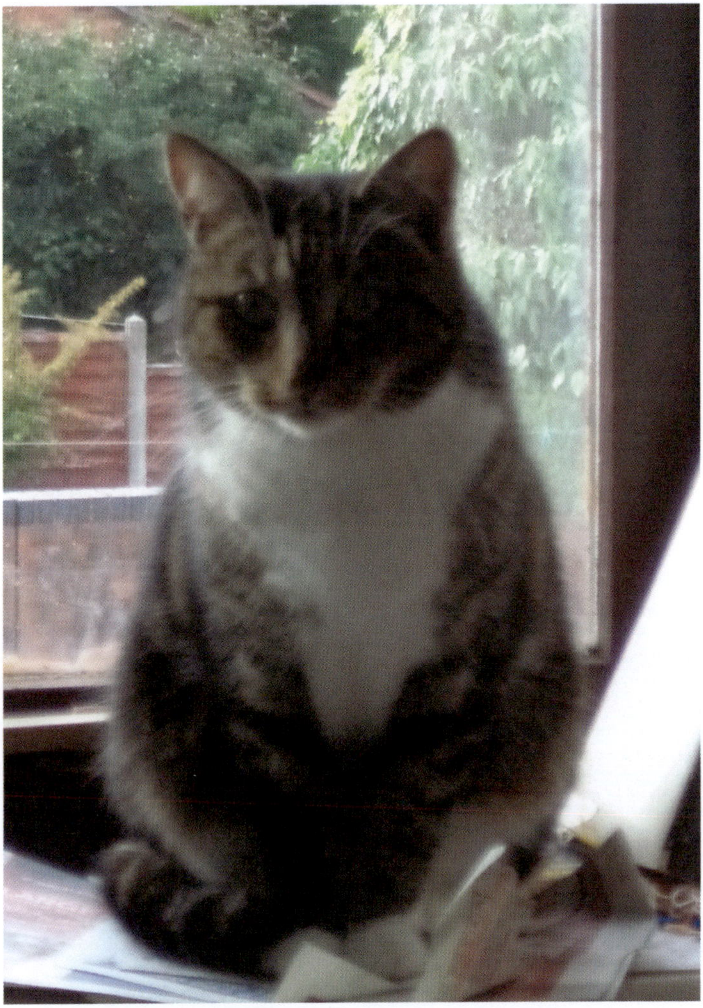

Printed in Great Britain
by Amazon